FOCUS ON PRONUNCIATION 3

LINDA LANE

American Language Program
Columbia University

Focus on Pronunciation 3

Pearson Education, 10 Bank Street, White Plains, NY 10606

Executive editor: Laura Le Dréan
Development editor: Dena Daniel/Dana Klinek
Marketing manager: Joe Chapple
Production coordinator: Melissa Leyva
Production editor: Helen Ambrosio
Senior manufacturing buyer: Nancy Flaggman
Cover and text design: Pat Wosczyk
Cover photo: © Dimitri Veritsiotis/Digital Vision, Ltd.
Project management and text composition: Elm Street Publishing Services, Inc.
Text font: 11.5/13 Minion
Pronunciation diagrams: Tracey Cataldo
Text art: Jill Wood

Library of Congress Cataloging-in-Publication Data

Lane, Linda (Linda L.)
Focus on pronunciation. 3 / Linda Lane.
p. cm.
ISBN 0-13-097879-5
1. English language—Pronunciation—Problems, exercises, etc. 2. English language—Textbooks for foreign speakers. I. Title: FOP1. II. Title.
PE1137.L22 2005
428.3'4—dc22 2004008145

ISBN: 0-13-097879-5

Printed in the United States of America
7 8 9 10 11—V004—13 12 11 10

CONTENTS

INTRODUCTION

About *Focus on Pronunciation 3*

Focus on Pronunciation 3 is a comprehensive course that helps advanced students speak English more clearly and accurately. The course covers all aspects of pronunciation—sounds, stress, rhythm, and intonation.

Organization of *Focus on Pronunciation 3*

The units of *Focus on Pronunciation 3* are organized in five parts: Vowels, Consonants, Syllables and Stress within Words, Rhythm, and Intonation. Each part begins with an overview unit. The overview unit presents important topics included in that part. The units following the overview deal in depth with specific pronunciation points.

The Self-Study section provides listening and pronunciation practice. It usually includes one or more controlled exercises and a freer speaking task. This section is to be recorded by the student for the teacher to review and comment on.

Unit Organization

The units following the overviews typically have the following organization:

Introduction

The Introduction presents and explains the pronunciation point. It may show how sounds are made or present other useful information on the pronunciation point. Its purpose is to make students aware of the pronunciation point.

Focused Practice

This section contains classroom practice activities. The activities are designed to ensure student involvement through games, interactive tasks, and listening/speaking activities dealing with high-interest topics.

- Students first work on controlled activities that allow them to develop skill and proficiency with the particular point.
- They then practice the point in freer, communicative activities. When students are engaged in freer activities, they should be encouraged to keep in mind these global features of clear speaking:
  - Speak Slowly
  - Speak Loudly Enough
  - Pay Attention to the Ends of Words
  - Use Your Voice to Speak Expressively
- Each unit has one or more activities dealing with a particular theme or content area.

Audio

The Classroom audio program for *Focus on Pronunciation 3* has all the recorded activities for the course. In addition, there are Student CDs containing the Self-Study exercises.

Key to Icons

—material recorded on the full audio program

—material recorded on the Student CDs

—pair activity

—group activity

—material for students to record and give to the teacher

Planning a Syllabus

The units in *Focus on Pronunciation 3* can be used in any order. In my own teaching, I like to "skip around"—for example, teaching the overview unit for Vowels, then a specific vowel unit, then the overview for Syllables and Stress within Words, then a specific unit on stress in words, and so on. Teachers who adopt this approach could also cover all the overview units at the beginning of the course and then skip around within the sections. The units can also be taught in order, first covering vowels, then consonants, and so on.

References

The following research influenced the content and method of this book.

Avery, Peter and S. Ehrlich. *Teaching American English Pronunciation.* Oxford: Oxford University Press, 1992.

Celce-Murcia, Marianne, D. M. Brinton, and J. M. Goodwin. *Teaching Pronunciation: A Reference for Teachers of English to Speakers of Other Languages.* Cambridge: Cambridge University Press, 1996.

Dauer, Rebecca. *Accurate English.* Prentice Hall Regents, 1993.

Acknowledgments

I am indebted to a number of people whose support, patience, and good humor made this book possible. I am grateful for the help and suggestions of my editors at Pearson: Ginny Blanford, Laura Le Dréan, Dena Daniel, and Helen Ambrosio.

I am grateful for the insightful comments and suggestions of the reviewers: Cindy Chang, University of Washington, Seattle, WA; Ninah Beliavsky, St. John's University, Jamaica, NY; Lauren Randolph, Rutgers University, Piscataway, NJ; Robert Baldwin, UCLA, Los Angeles, CA.

I would also like to express my thanks to my colleagues at the American Language Program at Columbia University, who used these materials in their own classes, for their advice and feedback.

For the encouragement and patience of my family, Mile, Martha, Sonia, and Luke, and of my dear friend Mary Jerome, I am deeply grateful.

Finally, I want to thank my students—for teaching me how they learn pronunciation, for wanting to improve their pronunciation, and for showing me how to help them.

Linda Lane

ABOUT THE AUTHOR

Linda Lane is a faculty member in the American Language Program of Columbia University. She is coordinator of Columbia's TESOL Certificate Program, where she also teaches Applied Phonetics and Pronunciation Teaching and Introduction to Second Language Acquisition. She received her Ed.D. in Applied Linguistics from Teachers College, Columbia University, and her M.A. in Linguistics from Yale University.

VOWELS

UNIT 1 Vowel overview

THE VOWELS OF AMERICAN ENGLISH

There are fourteen vowel sounds in American English: eleven vowels and three complex vowels. Vowels are produced by movements of the tongue up and down, and front and back.

1 THE VOWELS OF ENGLISH

VOWEL CHART
TONGUE POSITIONS OF THE VOWELS OF ENGLISH

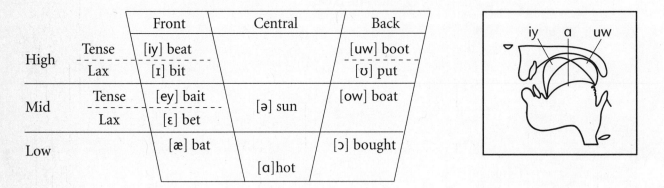

		Front	Central	Back
High	Tense	[iy] beat		[uw] boot
	Lax	[ɪ] bit		[ʊ] put
Mid	Tense	[ey] bait	[ə] sun	[ow] boat
	Lax	[ɛ] bet		
Low		[æ] bat	[ɑ]hot	[ɔ] bought

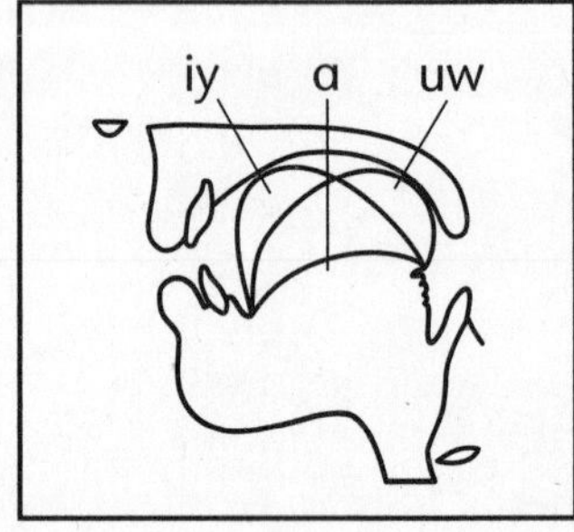

COMPLEX VOWELS

[aw] how   [ay] high   [oy] boy

- The columns in the vowel chart show whether the tongue is toward the front, center, or back of the mouth.
- The rows show whether the tongue is high, in the middle, or low in the mouth.
- The drawing of the mouth shows the approximate position for three of the vowels.

A. Listen to the recording and repeat the vowel sounds and sample words.

B. Listen again and circle the vowels that sound similar to vowels in your language. Put a check next to the vowels that you think may be difficult for you.

2 FEELING SOUNDS

 Work with a partner to do these vowel experiments.

A. Front and Back Vowels. The vowel in *be* [iy] is a front vowel; the vowel in *do* [uw] is a back vowel.

Say [iy-uw-iy-uw]

Concentrate on your tongue—feel it move from front to back (it may be easier to feel the movement if you close your eyes as you speak).

Say [ey-ow-ey-ow] (the vowels in *day* and *go*)

What happens to your lips when you move from front vowels ([iy] or [ey]) to back vowels ([uw] or [ow])?

B. High and Low Vowels. The vowel in *be* [iy] is a high vowel. The vowel in *hot* [ɑ] is a low vowel.

Say [iy-ɑ-iy-ɑ]

Feel the tongue moving up and down (or, feel your jaw opening and closing).

Say [uw-ɑ-uw-ɑ] (the vowels in *do* and *hot*).

What happens to your lips when you move from [uw] to [ɑ]?

GROUPS OF VOWELS

➤ TENSE AND LAX VOWELS

Tense and lax vowel pairs, like *feet-fit*, are difficult for many students. Tense vowels are pronounced with more muscle tension. With lax vowels, the muscles of the mouth are more relaxed.

Tense vowels: [iy] ***see***, [ey] ***pay***, [ow] ***grow***, [uw] ***shoe***
• **Many languages have vowels that are similar to these vowels.** • **In English, the tense vowels are not *pure* vowels—they end in [y] or [w].**
Lax vowels: [ɪ] ***thin***, [ɛ] ***bread***, [ʊ] ***would***
• **These are new vowels for many students.**

3 HEARING AND SEEING DIFFERENCES

Look at the diagrams of the vowel pairs.

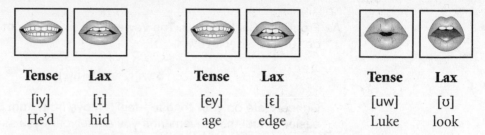

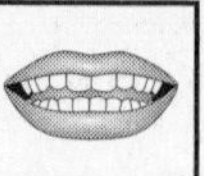    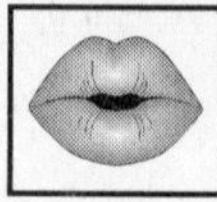 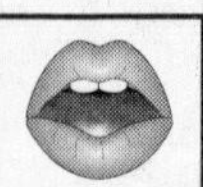

Tense	**Lax**	**Tense**	**Lax**	**Tense**	**Lax**
[iy]	[ɪ]	[ey]	[ɛ]	[uw]	[ʊ]
He'd	hid	age	edge	Luke	look

Notice that for the lax vowel, the mouth looks more relaxed and the lips are less spread and less rounded. The muscles inside the mouth are also more relaxed.

A. Listen to the tense-lax pairs and repeat them. Say the tense vowel first. Then let your tongue drop a little to the center of your mouth and say the lax vowel. Keep your lips relaxed for the lax vowel. Then listen again and circle the word you hear.

Tense	**Lax**	**Tense**	**Lax**	**Tense**	**Lax**
1. a. [iy]	**b.** [ɪ]	**5. a.** [ey]	**b.** [ɛ]	**9. a.** [uw]	**b.** [ʊ]
2. a. each	**b.** itch	**6. a.** wait	**b.** wet	**10. a.** Luke	**b.** look
3. a. leave	**b.** live	**7. a.** paper	**b.** pepper	**11. a.** who'd	**b.** hood
4. a. sleep	**b.** slip	**8. a.** faints	**b.** fence	**12. a.** stewed*	**b.** stood

**stewed:* meat and vegetables cooked slowly in liquid

B. Work with a partner and take turns. Choose a word from Part A and say it to your partner. Pronounce the vowel carefully so your partner can tell you which word you said.

4 Words With [ɛ], [æ], [ə], and [ɑ]

Look at the mouth diagrams for the vowels.

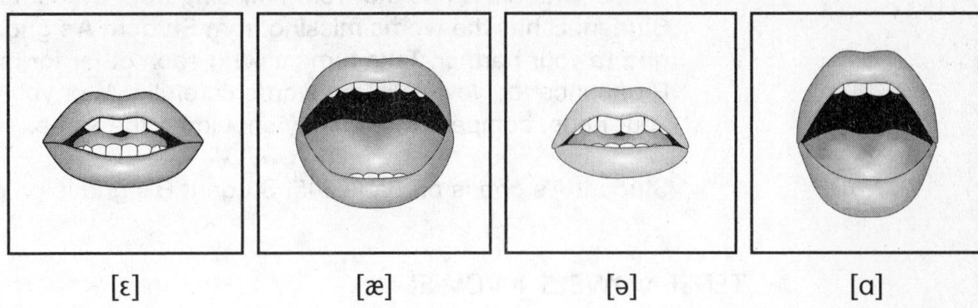

The vowels in *head, had, hut,* and *hot* are difficult for many students. These vowels are pronounced in the front or center of the mouth, with the tongue in the middle of the mouth or low in the mouth.

- The lips are spread for the vowels in *head* and *had.*
- The lips are not spread for the vowels in *hut* and *hot.*
- The mouth is open for the vowels in *had* and *hot.*
- The mouth is more closed for the vowels in *head* and *hut.*

A. Look at the mouth diagrams as you listen to the words and repeat them.

[ɛ]	[æ]	[ə]	[ɑ]
1. a. pet	**b.** pat	**c.** putt*	**d.** pot
2. a. wren*	**b.** ran	**c.** run	**d.** Ron
3. a. net	**b.** Nat	**c.** nut	**d.** not

**putt:* the short shot in golf; *wren:* a small bird

B. Work with a partner. Choose a word from Part A and say it to your partner. Use the diagrams to help you. Pronounce the vowel carefully so your partner can tell you which word you said.

5 FILL IN THE GRID

Work with a partner. Each of you has a grid that is partially filled in with words. Student A has the words missing from Student B's grid, and Student B has the words missing from Student A's grid. Don't show your grid to your partner. Take turns asking each other for missing words. Pronounce the vowels in the words carefully. After you both complete your grids, compare them. They should be the same.

Student A's grid is on page 245. Student B's grid is on page 251.

➤ TENSE VOWELS + VOWEL

When a tense vowel ([iy], [ey], [ow], or [uw]) is followed by another vowel, join the vowels together with [w] or [y].

grow‿up pay‿it

6 JOINING VOWELS

A. Listen to the recording and fill in the blanks. The first word ends with the vowel [iy], [ey], [ow], or [uw]. The next word begins with a vowel. The two words are joined together with [y] or [w].

1. **A:** The clock—can you ____________ ____________?
   B: Yes. It's ____________ ____________.
2. **A:** Let's go to the beach on your ____________ ____________.
   B: I'd rather ____________ ____________ home and sleep.
3. **A:** Why don't you want to ____________ ____________ with me?
   B: You never ____________ ____________ when you say you will.
4. **A:** How did you ____________ ____________ the test?
   B: I got ____________ ____________ wrong.

B. Compare your answers with a partner, and then practice the dialogues.

UNIT 2 [iy] sleep and [ɪ] slip

INTRODUCTION

➤ THE VOWELS

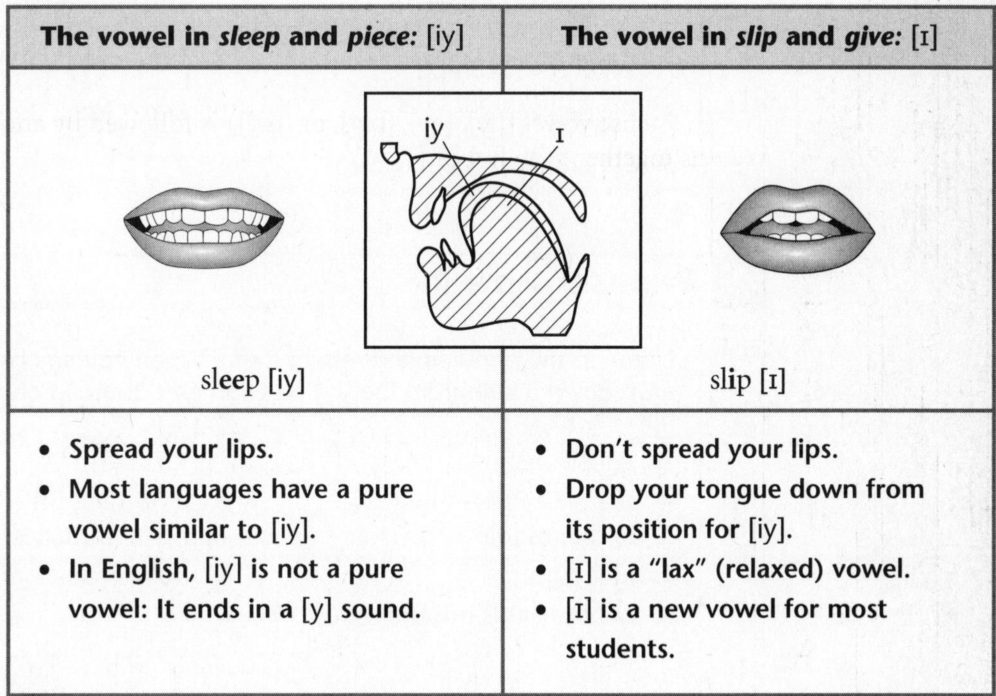

The vowel in *sleep* and *piece:* [iy]	The vowel in *slip* and *give:* [ɪ]
sleep [iy]	slip [ɪ]
• Spread your lips. • Most languages have a pure vowel similar to [iy]. • In English, [iy] is not a pure vowel: It ends in a [y] sound.	• Don't spread your lips. • Drop your tongue down from its position for [iy]. • [ɪ] is a "lax" (relaxed) vowel. • [ɪ] is a new vowel for most students.

➤ JOINING [iy] TO FOLLOWING VOWELS

When [iy] is followed by another vowel, use [y] to join the two vowels together. The vowels are in different syllables.

radi^{y}o   be^{y}open

FOCUSED PRACTICE

1 PHRASES WITH [iy]

Listen to the phrases and repeat them. Be sure to pronounce [y]. When [iy] is followed by another vowel, use [y] to join the vowels together. (The letter "y" has been added to help you.)

1. a deep sleep
2. a week at the beach
3. Eastern people
4. Please keep it.
5. Let's meet at the muse^y^um
6. It seems easy.
7. Did you see^y^ it?
8. When will the meeting be^y^ over?
9. Don't leave the key in the door.

2 PHRASES WITH [ɪ]

Listen to the phrases and repeat them. When you say [ɪ], let your tongue drop down a little from the [iy] position and don't spread your lips.

1. six sick women
2. gift-giving traditions
3. in the middle
4. in a minute
5. Bill built this building.
6. a big dinner
7. a slippery hill
8. My chin itches.
9. busy businessmen

3 HEARING DIFFERENCES

A. Listen to the phrases and repeat them. Then listen again and circle the phrase you hear.

1. **a.** sleep a lot
   b. slip a lot
2. **a.** Heat it.
   b. Hit it.
3. **a.** good feet
   b. good fit
4. **a.** I've got a bad feeling.
   b. I've got a bad filling.*
5. **a.** the son's reason
   b. The sun's risen.
6. **a.** cheap containers
   b. chip containers

**filling:* dental work that fills a decayed spot in a tooth

B. Work with a partner and take turns. Choose a phrase from Part A and say it to your partner. Pronounce the vowels carefully so your partner can tell you which phrase you said.

4 DIFFERENCES IN MEANING

Work with a partner and take turns. Read either sentence *a* or sentence *b* to your partner. Pronounce the underlined word carefully so your partner can read the correct response to you.

Sentence	Response
1. a. He has to live there.	That's too bad. It's a terrible neighborhood.
b. He has to leave there.	That's too bad. He seemed so happy in that job.
2. a. He has a sheep.	I've heard they make good pets.
b. He has a ship.	I thought he was afraid of the water.
3. a. Fill the glass.	With water?
b. Feel the glass.	It's very smooth.
4. a. He got the least of the winners.	Really? He deserved to get the most!
b. He got the list of the winners.	Is my name on it?

5 FILL IN THE GRID

Work with a partner. Each of you has a grid that is partially filled in with words. Student A has the words missing from Student B's grid, and Student B has the words missing from Student A's grid. Don't show your grid to your partner. Take turns asking each other for missing words. Pronounce the vowels in the words carefully. After you both complete your grids, compare them. They should be the same.

Student A's grid is on page 245. Student B's grid is on page 251.

6 LISTENING: *"A Gift for Him"*

A. Listen to the recording and fill in the blanks. All of the missing words have the vowels [ɪ] or [iy].

It's ______________ again—a time when ______________ panic over what to ______________ their men—a time when men ______________ to analyze the ______________ of their ______________. The ______________ ______________ ______________ to men are often good ______________ of how women ______________ about their men and the relationship.

B. Compare your answers with a partner. Did you hear the same words? If not, discuss which answer is probably right. Then practice reading the passage to each other. Be sure to pronounce the vowels carefully.

7 GOOD GIFT OR BAD GIFT?

The twelve gifts in this chart are gifts that women have given to the special men in their lives. According to AskMen.com's Web site, six of the gifts are good gifts and six are bad gifts.

Work with a partner. Which gifts do you think are "good gifts" and which are "bad gifts"? What makes them good or bad? (See page 243 for AskMen.com's classification.)

Gifts for men	Good or bad?	Reason
Tickets to see his favorite team play		
A tie		
Something he can use for his favorite hobby		
Tools		
Opera tickets		

Gifts for men	Good or bad?	Reason
Silver cuff links		
A picture of her		
Race-car driving lessons		
A book from the best-seller list		
An electric razor		
White socks		
A sweater		

First listen to:

- Exercises 1, 2, and 3.

Now record them.

Think of three people you give gifts to. Make a one-minute recording answering these questions about each of them:

Is it easy or difficult to find this person a gift? Why?
What do you usually give him or her?
What is the last gift you gave to this person?
Do you think he or she liked it?

UNIT 3 [ey] wait, [ɛ] wet, and [ɪ] wit Alternating vowels: [iy] ~ [ɛ]

INTRODUCTION

➤ THE VOWELS

The vowel in ***wait* and *stay*:** [ey]	The vowel in ***wet* and *ten*:** [ɛ]	The vowel in ***wit* and *live*:** [ɪ]
late [ey]	let [ɛ]	lit [ɪ]
• **Spread your lips.** • **[ey] ends in a [y] sound.**	• **Start with [ey]. Let your tongue drop down a little.** • **Spread your lips just a little.** • **Relax your tongue, your lips, and your cheeks.** **[ɛ] is a lax vowel.**	• **Start with [iy], the vowel in *eat*. Let your tongue drop down a little.** • **Don't spread your lips.** • **The tongue is a little higher in the mouth for [ɪ] than for [ɛ]. [ɪ] is a lax vowel.**

➤ JOINING [ey] TO A FOLLOWING VOWEL

When another vowel follows [ey], use [y] to join the two vowels together. The vowels are in different syllables.

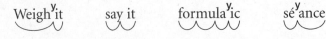

say it formula^y ic sé^y ance

➤ ALTERNATING VOWELS

In some related pairs of words, the stressed vowel alternates between [iy] and [ɛ]:

meter ~ metric keep ~ kept

FOCUSED PRACTICE

1 PHRASES WITH [ey], [ɛ], AND [ɪ]

Listen to the phrases and repeat them. The bold letters are [ey], [ɛ], or [ɪ]. Join [ey] to following vowels. Join final consonants to following vowels.

[ey]	[ɛ]	[ɪ]
1. take a train	4. my best friend	7. single women
2. explain our mistakes	5. wet weather	8. Which wish?
3. stay out late	6. credit card debt	9. busy businessmen

2 HEARING DIFFERENCES

A. Listen to the phrases and repeat them. Then listen again and circle the phrase you hear.

1. a. Rake it.
   b. Wreck it.
2. a. Savor it.*
   b. Sever it.*
3. a. I spilled milk.
   b. I spelled "milk."
4. a. a trained setter.*
   b. a trendsetter*
5. a. a better butter
   b. a bitter butter
6. a. the age of the universe
   b. the edge of the universe

**savor:* to enjoy something (usually a taste); *sever:* to cut; *setter:* breed of dog; *trendsetter:* someone who creates ("sets") new trends

B. Work with a partner and take turns. Choose a phrase from Part A and say it to your partner. Pronounce the vowels carefully so your partner can tell you which phrase you said.

3 DIFFERENCES IN MEANING

Work with a partner and take turns. Read either sentence *a* or sentence *b* to your partner. Pronounce the underlined word carefully so your partner can read the correct response to you.

Sentence	Response
1. a. He can't write with the pain.	Maybe he should see a doctor.
b. He can't write with the pen.	Is it out of ink?

continued

Sentence	Response
2. a. We're going to have a little test now.	I wish I'd studied last night.
b. We're going to have a little taste now.	Oh, good. I love chocolate.
3. a. He has a lot of debts.	Credit cards can be very dangerous.
b. He has a lot of dates.	I wish my social life were as active!
4. a. Let's weight the branches down.	I'll put these rocks on them.
b. Let's wet the branches down.	They do look awfully dry.

4 ALTERNATING VOWELS

In some related words, the stressed vowel alternates between [iy] and [ɛ]. The vowel in the more basic word is usually [iy].

A. Listen to the words and repeat them.

[iy]	[ɛ]
1. a. meter	b. metric
2. a. sleep	b. slept
3. a. sincere	b. sincerity
4. a. brief	b. brevity
5. a. serene	b. serenity
6. a. deceive	b. deception
7. a. receive	b. reception

B. With a partner, pronounce these pairs of words and decide whether the bold letters are alternating vowels or the same vowel. If they are alternating vowels, write "A" in the blank. If they are the same, write "S" in the blank.

1. please—pleasant A
2. reason—reasonable ___
3. discreet—discretion ___
4. delete—deletion ___
5. please—pleasure ___
6. compete—competitive ___
7. secret—secretive ___
8. heal—health ___

FRIENDS TO THE END

5 QUOTATIONS

A. Listen to the quotes about friendship and fill in the blanks. The missing words have [ey], [ɛ], or [ɪ] vowels.

1. A real ____________ is one who walks ____________ ____________ others walk out.
2. A friend is someone who believes in you ____________ you have ceased to believe ____________ ____________.
3. Lots of people want to ride with you in the limo,* but what you want is someone who will ____________ the bus with you ____________ the limo ____________ down.
4. When it hurts to look back, and you're ____________ to look ____________, you can look beside you, and your ____________ friend will be ____________.
5. ____________ and your friends feel superior. Succeed and ____________ feel ____________.
6. The statistics on sanity are that one out of ____________ four ____________ is suffering from some form of ____________ ____________. ____________ of your three best friends. If ____________ OK, ____________ it's you.

*_limo:_ short for "limousine"

B. Compare your answers with a partner, and then practice reading the quotations to each other. Which quotations do you think are meant to be humorous? Which ones are serious?

6 LISTENING: *"Friends"*

A. Before you listen, make sure you understand this vocabulary.

network	tangible	sounding board	coping	buffer

B. Listen to the passage on friendship. Take notes on the types of support friends provide.

Type of support	Examples
1.	
2.	
3.	

C. Now listen to three people describe how their friends helped them. What type(s) of support do the friends provide?

1. Mary ____________________
2. Joe ____________________
3. Beth ____________________

D. As a class or in small groups, discuss these questions:

1. Of the three types of support mentioned in the recording, which type do you think is most common in friendships? Why?
2. Do you have friends who would provide all three types of support?
3. Do you think some types of support are more likely to be provided by family rather than friends? Why?

First listen to:

- Exercises 1 and 2.

Now record them.

Make a one-minute recording about a good friend of yours.
How long have you been friends? What do you like to do together?
How do you and your friend help each other?

UNIT 4 [æ] man and [ɛ] men
Alternating vowels: [ey] ~ [æ]

INTRODUCTION

➤ THE VOWELS

The vowel in *man* and *happen:* [æ]	The vowel in *men* and *head:* [ɛ]
man [æ]	men [ɛ]
• Open your mouth and spread your lips. • The tip of your tongue is behind the lower teeth, pushing down and slightly forward.	• Your mouth is less open and more relaxed for [ɛ] than for [æ].

➤ ALTERNATING VOWELS

In some pairs of related words, the stressed vowel alternates between [ey] and [æ].

sane ~ sanity   stable ~ establish

FOCUSED PRACTICE

1 PHRASES WITH [æ] AND [ɛ]

Listen to the phrases and repeat them.

[æ]	[ɛ]
1. a bad example	**5.** precious metals
2. a ham sandwich	**6.** deli menu
3. natural reaction	**7.** heavy schedule
4. fast food	**8.** heaven and hell

2 THE [æ]-[ɛ] GAME

Divide the class into two groups, Team 1 and Team 2. Team 1 asks questions of Team 2, and vice versa. All of the questions can be answered with a common [æ] or [ɛ] word. The team that is answering questions receives a point for each correct answer, correctly pronounced.

EXAMPLE

Team 1: What's another way of saying "50 percent"?

Team 2: *half*

Team 1's questions are on page 245; Team 2's questions are on page 251.

3 SENTENCES FULL OF SOUNDS

A. Listen to the sentences and repeat them. Group words together and pronounce the vowels carefully.

1. Ten tan tennis players attempted to take the champion's racket.
2. The cook blended a breakfast drink of bananas and bran in the black blender, but it was too bland to drink.
3. The experts expended a lot of energy creating a plan for the bridge expansion.

B. Practice the sentences with a partner. Then choose one of the sentences to say to the class. Speak as smoothly as you can.

4 ALTERNATING VOWELS

- In some related words, the stressed vowel alternates between [æ] and [ey]. The vowel in the more basic word is usually [ey].

A. Listen to the words and repeat them.

	[ey]	[æ]		[ey]	[æ]
1.	sane	sanity	**5.**	nature	natural
2.	shade	shadow	**6.**	nation	national
3.	grateful	gratitude	**7.**	grain	granular
4.	depraved	depravity	**8.**	exclaim	exclamatory

B. With a partner, pronounce these pairs of words and decide whether the bold letters are alternating vowels or the same vowel. If they are alternating vowels, write "A" in the blank. If they are the same, write "S" in the blank.

1. grave—gravity A
2. space—spatial ___
3. fame—famous ___
4. state—static ___
5. brave—bravery ___
6. grade—gradual ___
7. bathe—bath ___
8. station—stationary ___
9. cave—cavity ___
10. explain—explanatory ___
11. escape—escapist ___
12. behave—behavior ___

HEALTH AND HEAVINESS

5 LISTENING: *"Lighten up, Brooklyn"*

A. Before you listen, make sure you understand this vocabulary.

challenge	campaign	pit	neighbor
against	shrunk	collective	

B. Listen to "Lighten up, Brooklyn" and fill in the information.

Length of diet ______________ Weight-loss goal ______________

Actual weight loss ______________ Number of winners ______________

Winners' weight loss ______________ Winners' prize ______________

6 Determining Causes

Health organizations are increasingly concerned about the growing number of overweight people in the world. The causes for this problem are complex, involving lifestyle, diet, education, standard of living, and genetics.

A. The list shows some of the causes cited for overweight and obesity. Check the three that you think are most responsible for these problems. The bold letters are [æ] or [ɛ].

1. eating too much fat ___

2. taking in too many calories ___

3. eating too much sugar ___

4. eating too much fast food ___

5. lack of exercise ___

6. watching too much TV ___

7. lack of information ___

8. genetic propensity ___

9. poverty ___

10. wealth ___

Other ____________ ___

B. Compare the causes you checked with your classmates. Do you agree? Talk about your choices and listen while others explain their opinions. Look at the list again. Would you check the same three causes now?

First listen to:

- Exercise 1.

Now record it.

Make a one-minute recording discussing the reasons you think that overweight and obesity are becoming a global health problem.

UNIT 5 [ɑ] lock and [ə] luck Reduction of unstressed vowels

INTRODUCTION

➤ THE VOWELS

The vowel in *lock* and *father:* [ɑ]	The vowel in *luck* and *money:* [ə]
lock [ɑ]	luck [ə]
• Your mouth is open. • The tip of your tongue rests in the bottom of your mouth. • Your lips are not rounded.	• Your tongue rests in the center of your mouth. • Your lips should be relaxed and open only a little.

[ə] is the "hesitation" sound of English, usually written *uh.*

It's . . . uh [ə] *. . . uh* [ə] *. . . it's . . . uh* [ə] *. . . I'm sure it's here somewhere.*

Most unstressed vowels are pronounced [ə], making it the most common vowel in English.

əgó (ago)   əccúr (occur)   ópən (open)   əbándən (abandon)

FOCUSED PRACTICE

1 PHRASES WITH [ɑ] AND [ə]

Listen to the phrases and repeat them. The bold vowels are [ɑ] or [ə]. Your mouth should be open for [ɑ] and nearly closed for [ə].

[ɑ]	[ə]
1. m**o**dern techn**o**logy	5. en**ou**gh m**o**ney
2. **o**dd j**o**bs	6. corr**u**pt g**o**vernment
3. the he**a**rt of the pr**o**blem	7. **o**nce a m**o**nth
4. p**o**pular p**o**licy	8. br**o**therly l**o**ve

2 HEARING DIFFERENCES

Listen to the words and repeat them. Then listen again and circle the word you hear.

1. a. soccer
   b. succor*
2. a. body
   b. buddy
3. a. blonder
   b. blunder*
4. a. collar**
   b. color
5. a. hog*
   b. hug
6. a. wants
   b. once

**succor:* help; *blunder:* mistake; *hog:* large male pig
**Some people pronounce *collar* with the [ɔ] vowel.

3 SOUNDS AND SPELLING

Listen to the pairs of words. If the bold vowels are the same in both words, write "S" in the blank. If they are different vowels, write "D" in the blank. Then circle the words that have [ə].

1. d**o**ne, b**o**ne D
2. l**o**ve, m**o**ve ___
3. m**o**nkey, d**o**nkey ___
4. wh**a**t, h**a**t ___
5. d**oe**s, p**oe**t ___
6. h**o**ney, l**u**nch ___
7. **o**ther, n**o**thing ___
8. bl**oo**d, f**oo**d ___
9. c**ou**ple, fl**oo**d ___
10. t**ou**ch, d**u**ck ___
11. **o**nce, y**ou**ng ___
12. c**ou**sin, c**ou**gh ___

4 Unstressed Vowels

These words have been "respelled" to show how the unstressed vowels are pronounced. Listen to the words and repeat them. Then write the correct spelling of the word in the blank. (You can check the corrected spellings on page 243.)

1. pəséssəv	**4.** státəs	**7.** cəmmánd
possessive	______	______
2. ənnóuncemənt	**5.** pəllútəd	**8.** əppéarənce
______	______	______
3. hóstəl	**6.** bənánə	**9.** tənı́ght
______	______	______

MONEY, MONEY, MONEY!

5 Listening: *"Henrietta Howland Green: World's Most Notorious Miser"*

A. Before you listen, make sure you understand this vocabulary.

notorious	inherited	oatmeal
miser	amputated	died of a stroke

B. Listen to "Henrietta Howland Green: World's Most Notorious Miser." As you listen, keep count of the number of times you hear the word *money.* Listen again if you need to.

I heard *money* ______________ times.

C. Work with a partner and take turns asking and answering these questions. Use the word *money* in your answers. Remember that the first vowel in *money* is [ə].

1. What happened when Mrs. Green's father died?

____

2. Why did Mrs. Green's son have to have his leg amputated?

____

continued

3. Why did Mrs. Green eat only cold oatmeal?

____

4. What do you think happened to her money when she died?

____

6 CAN'T BUY ME LOVE

We use money to buy things we want and need, like food or clothes or a car. But we also use it to obtain intangibles, like independence, power, status, or security.

A. **Work with a partner and take turns. Each of you has statements from three people who use money to obtain one of the intangibles in the box. Read one of your statements out loud. Your partner will decide which intangible the statement refers to. Do you agree? Could it refer to another intangible as well?**

love/friendship	power	status
loyalty	security	independence

Student A's statements are on page 245; Student B's statements are on page 251.

B. **Discuss this question with your partner: If you had all the money you could ever want, what would you do with it?**

First listen to:

- Exercises 1 and 2.

Now record them.

Make a one-minute recording about money. How important is money to you? What do you think of people who are very rich? If you suddenly had a lot of money, do you think it would change you?

UNIT 6 [ɛ] head, [æ] had, [ə] hut, and [ɑ] hot Reductions: *-man, can, -body*

INTRODUCTION

➤ THE VOWELS

The vowel in ***head*** **and** ***said:*** [ɛ]	The vowel in ***had*** **and** ***sad:*** [æ]	The vowel in ***hut*** **and** ***mother:*** [ə]	The vowel in ***hot*** **and** ***heart:*** [ɑ]
head [ɛ]	had [æ]	hut [ə]	hot [ɑ]
See Unit 3.	**See Unit 4.**	**See Unit 5.**	**See Unit 5.**

➤ REDUCTIONS OF [æ] AND [ɑ]

When unstressed, these vowels are reduced to [ə] in some common words:

- *-man* and *-men* are pronounced [mən] in words like *fireman/firemen, chairman/chairmen, policeman/policemen.*
- *can* is pronounced [kən] before a verb: *She can* [kən] *dance.*
- *-body* sounds like "buddy" in *somebody, nobody, everybody,* and *anybody.*

FOCUSED PRACTICE

1 WORDS WITH [ɛ], [æ], [ə], AND [ɑ]

Listen to the words and repeat them. Then listen again and circle the words you hear.

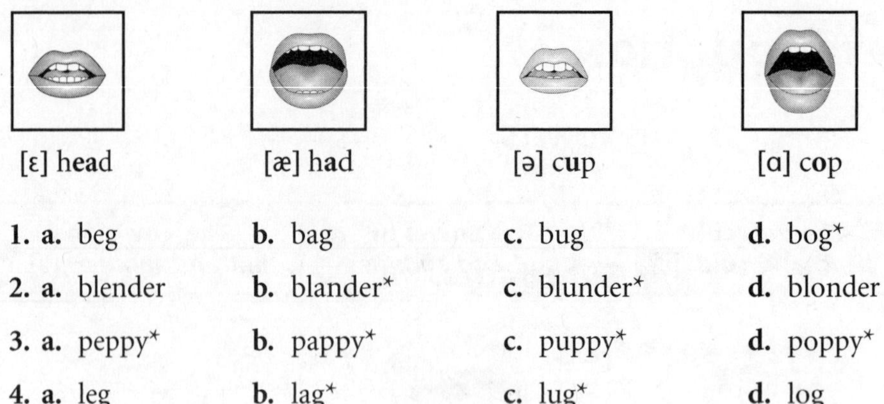

[ɛ] head	[æ] had	[ə] cup	[ɑ] cop
1. a. beg	**b.** bag	**c.** bug	**d.** bog*
2. a. blender	**b.** blander*	**c.** blunder*	**d.** blonder
3. a. peppy*	**b.** pappy*	**c.** puppy*	**d.** poppy*
4. a. leg	**b.** lag*	**c.** lug*	**d.** log

**bog:* land almost below water—marshland; *blander:* comparative of *bland*—plain; *blunder:* mistake; *peppy:* energetic; *pappy:* daddy (dialect); *puppy:* baby dog; *poppy:* large red flower; *lag:* follow behind; *lug:* carry something heavy

2 FILL IN THE GRID

Work with a partner. Each of you has a grid that is partially filled in with words. Student A has the words missing from Student B's grid, and Student B has the words missing from Student A's grid. Don't show your grid to your partner. Take turns asking each other for missing words. Pronounce the vowels in the words carefully. After you both complete your grids, compare them. They should be the same.

Student A's grid is on page 246. Student B's grid is on page 252.

3 DIFFERENCES IN MEANING

Work with a partner and take turns. Read either sentence *a* or sentence *b* to your partner. Pronounce the underlined word carefully so your partner can read the correct response to you.

Sentence	**Response**
1. a. There's a small red <u>bug</u> on the table.	It's a ladybug.
b. There's a small red <u>bag</u> on the table.	It's a present—open it!

Sentence	Response
2. a. What shall I do with this poppy?	Put it in a vase.
b. What shall I do with this puppy?	Feed it.
3. a. Bring me the green cup.	I'm drinking out of it.
b. Bring me the green cap.	It's too small for your head.
4. a. This is a new cut.	Playing with knives again?
b. This is a new cot.	Is it comfortable?

4 Dialogues

Listen to the dialogues and repeat the lines. Stress the capitalized words by pronouncing them louder and on a higher pitch. Remember to reduce the vowels in *can, -man/-men,* and *-body.* Then practice the dialogues with a partner.

1. A: Who's outSIDE?
B: NObody. It's just the WIND.
A: It SOUNDS like somebody's at the DOOR.
B: NO. It's NObody.
A: NO. I can HEAR somebody at the DOOR. Go CHECK.
B: Go BACK to sleep. There's NObody at the DOOR.

2. A: I THINK we're LOST. Let's STOP and ask for diRECtions.
B: There's nobody aROUND. Maybe we can find a GAS station and ask somebody THERE.
A: Everything seems to be CLOSED. I guess everybody in this TOWN goes to BED early.
B: If you start SPEEDing, I'm SURE we'll find a poLICEman. THEN we can ask for diRECtions.

WHAT IT TAKES TO GRADUATE

5 LISTENING: *"Graduation Requirements"*

A. Listen to the recording and fill in the blanks. The missing words have the vowels [ɛ], [æ], [ə], or [ɑ].

Most students devote a great deal of thought and ______________ to the ______________ of getting into ______________—getting out of college is something they think about later. Four-year colleges in the United States ______________ similar requirements for graduation. There is, of course, a requirement that all tuition and fees be paid before the degree is ______________.* Colleges also have a ______________ requirement: Most of the courses that count toward graduation ______________ be taken at the college granting the degree. This means that students who ______________ to ______________ to ______________ college should do so early, so they don't ______________ to take extra ______________ to fulfill the residency requirement.

*Some schools may allow students to graduate before all fees are paid if special arrangements are made.

B. Listen to the second part of the recording and take notes on the topics.

1. general education requirements

____

____

2. composition requirement

____

____

3. technology requirement

____

____

4. foreign language requirement

____

____

C. Work in small groups. Use your notes to summarize what was said about the requirements. Then discuss these questions:

1. For college students, what kinds of course requirements do (did) you have to fulfill, apart from your major courses?
2. What are the requirements for graduation from colleges in your country?

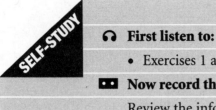

First listen to:

- Exercises 1 and 4.

Now record them.

Review the information from Exercise 5. Make a brief recording answering this question: Are the requirements for a college degree in your country similar to those in the United States? Explain the similarities and differences.

UNIT 7 Vowels followed by [r] The complex sound in *world*

INTRODUCTION

➤ [r] AFTER VOWELS

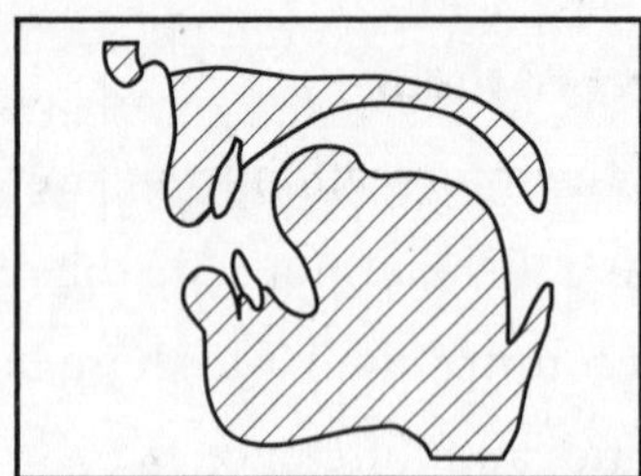

Turn the tip of your tongue up and slightly back.

➤ COMMON VOWELS BEFORE [r]

The sound in *her* and *first*: [ər]	**The sound in *or* and *door*: [or]**	**The sound in *are* and *hard*: [ɑr]**
[ər]	[or]	[ɑr]
• The mouth is almost closed. • The lips are slightly rounded. • Turn the tip of your tongue up and back.	• The lips are rounded. • Turn the tip of your tongue up and back.	• The mouth is open. • The lips are not rounded. • Turn the tip of your tongue up and back.

The sound in *world* and *girl*: [ərl] or [ərəl]
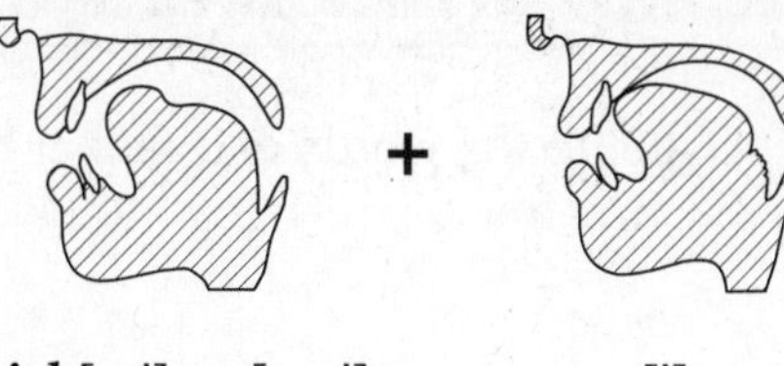 [r] **girl** [ərl] or [ərəl] + [l]

• **Your mouth is almost closed and your lips are a little rounded.**
• **Follow these two steps to say the sounds:**
  • **Turn the tip of your tongue up and back for [r].**
  • **It then touches behind the top teeth for [l].**
• **If this sound is difficult, pronounce it as two syllables joined together: [ərəl]**

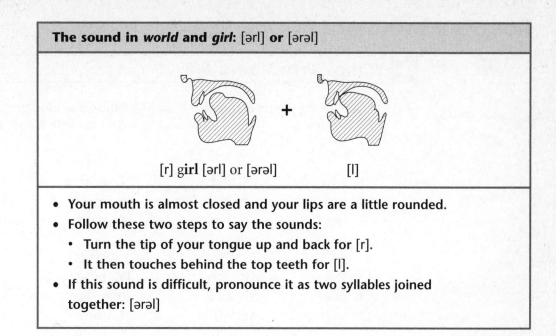

➤ SPELLINGS OF [ər]

This sound has several spellings.

Common spellings	***wor* + consonant**	**Less common spellings**
er serve	work word	*our* journey
ir first	worth worry	*ear* earth
ur hurt		

➤ DIALECTS

There are some dialects of American English that drop "r" after vowels, but not when the next word begins with a vowel. You should learn to pronounce [r] after vowels because most varieties of American English do not drop "r."

FOCUSED PRACTICE

1 WORDS WITH VOWEL + R

Listen to the words and repeat them. Turn the tip of your tongue up and back to make [r]. Then practice saying the words with a partner.

[ər]	[ɑr]	[ɪr]	[ɛr]
1. were	4. hard	7. hear	10. hair
2. first	5. far	8. fear	11. fair
3. heard	6. heart	9. near	12. wear

[or]	[ayər]	[awər]	[(y)ʊr]
13. tore	16. tire	19. hour	22. tour
14. pour	17. fire	20. tower	23. cure
15. war	18. hire	21. sour	24. pure

2 HEARING DIFFERENCES

A. Listen to the words and repeat them. Then listen again and circle the word you hear.

1. a. ear b. air	3. a. tore b. tour	5. a. heard b. hard	7. a. were b. war
2. a. far b. fur	4. a. bird b. beard	6. a. heart b. hurt	8. a. stir b. steer

B. Work with a partner and take turns. Choose a word from Part A and say it to your partner. Pronounce [r] and the vowel carefully so your partner can tell you which word you said.

3 SOUNDS AND SPELLING

Listen to these pairs of words. If the bold vowels are the same in both words, write "S" in the blank. If they are different, write "D" in the blank (see Appendix III).

1. furious, furriest D
2. accord, award ___
3. fierce, first ___
4. journey, church ___
5. beard, bird ___
6. weird, weary ___
7. regard, reward ___
8. heir, air ___
9. birthday, worthy ___
10. charming, warming ___

4 THE COMPLEX SOUND IN *WORLD*

Listen to the words and repeat them. Pronounce the bold sounds as two syllables: [ərəl].

1. wor**ld**
2. g**irl**
3. c**url**
4. wh**irl**
5. p**earl**
6. tw**irl**
7. the best in the wor**ld**
8. the whole wor**ld**
9. **world** leaders
10. **world**wide
11. **World** War II
12. **curl**y hair
13. **pearl** earrings
14. **girl**friend
15. **girls'** dormitory

FIRST PLACE

5 FIRST IN THE WORLD

These things hold first place in the world in their category. With a partner, decide what the category is for each thing. Then write a sentence using a superlative and ending with "in the world." Practice reading the sentences to each other. Be sure to pronounce *world* carefully.

1. the Nile River

   The Nile is the longest river in the world.

2. the Petronas Tower in Malaysia

   ____

3. the whale

   ____

4. China

   ____

5. Mount Everest

   ____

6. the cheetah

   ____

7. the Pacific Ocean

   ____

6 JEOPARDY: *Firsts*

Jeopardy is a game where the answers are known and you have to think of the questions.

You and your partner take turns being the *host* (the one who has the answers) and the *contestant* (the one who must provide the question). The category for this game is *Firsts*—people or places that were the first in some way.

Here's how to play:

- The contestant chooses an amount of points to risk in the category *Firsts.* The higher the amount, the greater the difficulty.
- The host reads the answer (the information) for that amount. (Be sure to pronounce "first" carefully.)
- The contestant has to say a question that makes sense for the answer the host just read.
- If the question is correct, the contestant earns the points assigned to that answer. If the question is incorrect, the contestant loses that amount.

EXAMPLE

B: *I'll take Firsts for 100.*

A: This country was the first to have a population of a billion people.

B: *What is China?*

A: That's correct! You win 100 points.

Student A's answers are on page 246. Student B's answers are on page 252.

First listen to:

- Exercises 1, 2, and 4.

Now record them.

Make a one-minute recording. Answer the questions using complete sentences. Pronounce words like *first* and *world* carefully.

1. What are three important problems facing the world today?
2. What leader has had a positive impact on the world? Why?
3. What leader has had a negative impact on the world? Why?

UNIT 8 [ow] boat, [ɔ] bought, and [ɑ] pot Alternating vowels: [ow] ~ [ɑ] Dialects

INTRODUCTION

➤ THE VOWELS

The vowel in *boat* and *show:* [ow]	The vowel in *bought* and *loss:* [ɔ]	The vowel in *pot* and *father:* [ɑ]
boat [ow]	bought [ɔ]	pot [ɑ]
• Start with your lips rounded. Continue rounding to make [ow]. • In many languages this vowel is a pure vowel [o]. In English, it ends with [w].	• Your mouth is open. • Your lips are slightly rounded. • This vowel is pronounced in the back of the mouth.	• Your mouth is open. • Your lips are not rounded. • Your tongue is in the low center of the mouth.

➤ JOINING [ow] TO VOWELS

When [ow] is followed by another vowel, use [w] to join the two sounds together. The two vowels are in different syllables.

po ʷ etry I have no ʷ idea.

➤ ALTERNATING VOWELS

In some pairs of related words, the stressed vowel alternates between [ow] and [ɑ].

know ~ knowledge   diagnosis ~ diagnostic

➤ DIALECTS

In British English, [ɔ] has more of an "o" sound than in American English. In American English, it has more of an [ɑ] sound. Many Americans from the West and Midwest, however, do not use the [ɔ] vowel. In these dialects, words like *bought* and *loss* are pronounced with [ɑ], the vowel in *father.* If you have difficulty pronouncing [ɔ], you can substitute [ɑ].

FOCUSED PRACTICE

1 PHRASES WITH [ow], [ɔ], AND [ɑ]

Listen to the phrases and repeat them.

[ow]	[ɔ]	[ɑ]
1. old clothes	**5.** an awful loss	**9.** top jobs
2. focus on goals	**6.** a long walk	**10.** a lot of knowledge
3. the whole show	**7.** a lost cause	**11.** stocks and bonds
4. I suppose so.	**8.** a cautious offer	**12.** a model economy

2 JOINING WORDS WITH [w]

In these phrases, [ow] is followed by another vowel. Listen carefully to the way the two words are joined together and repeat the phrases. (The letter "w" has been added to show the pronunciation.)

1. po^{w}etry
2. Chlo^{w}e
3. go^{w}out
4. I know it.
5. a show-off
6. bo^{w}a constrictor*
7. I have no^{w}answer.
8. a co^{w}op apartment
9. grow up

**boa constrictor:* large tropical snake

3 Dialect Differences

In the Northeast, some people pronounce *bought* and *pot* with different vowels. In the West and Midwest, most people pronounce both words with the vowel in *pot* [ɑ].

Listen to the difference in the pronunciation of these words. The first person is from Portland, Oregon. The second is from New York City.

1. thought
2. sorry
3. law
4. dawn
5. hall
6. long
7. caught
8. pause

4 Differences in Meaning

Work with a partner and take turns. Read either sentence *a* or sentence *b* to your partner. Pronounce the underlined word carefully so your partner can read the correct response to you.

Sentence	Response
1. a. I dropped the <u>ball</u>.	Did it bounce?
b. I dropped the <u>bowl</u>.	Did it break?
2. a. What a beautiful <u>fall</u>!	Yes, the trees are spectacular.
b. What a beautiful <u>foal</u>*!	Yes. Its mother is beautiful, too.
3. a. Why did he <u>sock</u>* the pillow?	It's part of his anger management therapy.
b. Why did he <u>soak</u> the pillow?	It was an accident—he spilled some water.
4. a. Why were you <u>cold</u>?	I left my coat at home.
b. Why were you <u>called</u>?	They want to interview me.

**foal:* a baby horse; *sock:* slang, to hit

5 Alternating Vowels

In some related words, the stressed vowel alternates between [ow] and [ɑ]. The vowel in the more basic word is usually [ow].

A. Listen to the words and repeat them.

	[ow]	[ɑ]
1.	joke	jocular
2.	evoke	evocative
3.	verbose	verbosity
4.	code	codify

B. With a partner, pronounce the pairs of words and decide whether the bold letters are alternating vowels or the same vowel. If they are alternating vowels, write "A" in the blank. If they are the same, write "S" in the blank.

1. s**o**lo—s**o**litude A
2. gr**ow**—gr**ow**th ___
3. h**o**ly—h**o**liday ___
4. er**o**de—er**o**sion ___
5. prom**o**te—prom**o**tion ___
6. cl**o**thing—cl**o**th ___
7. **o**men—**o**minous ___
8. expl**o**re—expl**o**ratory ___
9. kn**ow**—kn**ow**ledge ___
10. teleph**o**ne—teleph**o**nic ___

THE COLORS OF EMOTION

6 Listening: *"Emotional Responses to Color"*

A. Listen to the vocabulary words and repeat them. Make sure you understand what they mean. Then write each word in the row that corresponds to the sound of the bold vowels.

em**o**tional response	prom**o**te	a c**o**nflict
res**o**lve	fl**ow**	auton**o**mic (nervous system)
exh**au**sted	h**a**rmony	

[ow] g**o** ______________________

[ɔ] l**o**ss ______________________

[ɑ] st**o**p ______________________

B. Listen to the recording "Emotional Responses to Color." As you listen, write the emotional response connected to each of the colors in the chart. Then discuss your answers with a partner.

Color	Emotional response
Blue	
Green	
Orange	
Red	
Bright yellow	
Pale yellow	

First listen to:

- Exercises 1 and 2.

Now record them.

Review the information in Exercise 6B. Make a one-minute recording about the colors you would suggest for the following:

- **a.** a hospital
- **b.** a person who wants to lose weight
- **c.** someone who has trouble controlling anger
- **d.** someone who frequently feels confused
- **e.** a person who has low self-esteem

UNIT 9 [uw] cool, [ʊ] could, and [yuw] cute Alternating vowels: [uw/yuw] ~ [ə] The sequence [wʊ] woman

INTRODUCTION

➤ THE VOWELS

The vowel in *cool* and *shoe:* [uw]	The vowel in *could* and *good:* [ʊ]
cool [uw]	could [ʊ]
• Start with your lips rounded and continue rounding to make [uw]. • [uw] ends in a [w].	• Your lips are less rounded. • Your tongue drops a little toward the center of your mouth for [ʊ] compared with [uw].

➤ ALTERNATING VOWELS

In some pairs of related words, the stressed vowel alternates between [uw]/[yuw] and [ə].

ass**u**me ~ ass**u**mption   ded**u**ce ~ ded**u**ction

➤ SPELLING, SOUNDS, AND GRAMMAR

The first sound in words like *union* or *united* is the consonant [y]. Use the article *a* with these words (compare: *an umbrella* but *a union*).

➤ WORDS WITH [uw] OR [ʊ]

A few words can be pronounced with [uw] or [ʊ].

roof hoof root

➤ THE SEQUENCE [wʊ]

Some students have trouble pronouncing [w] when the next sound is [ʊ]. Their pronunciation of *woman* may sound like *'oman.* If this is a problem for you, try this:

- Start with your lips very rounded. Unround them a little (unrounding creates the beginning [w] sound):

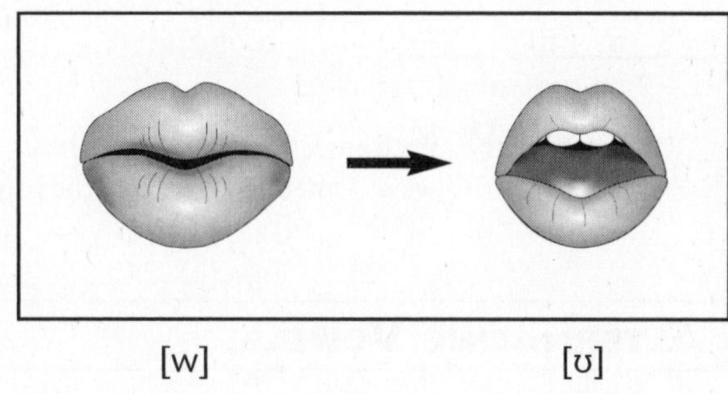

[w] [ʊ]

- Try saying two [u] sounds together: uuman (*woman*), uud (*wood*).
- Stretch a rubber band as you say the first part of *woman.*

FOCUSED PRACTICE

1 PHRASES WITH [uw]/[yuw], [ʊ], AND [wʊ]

Listen to the phrases and repeat them.

[uw] / [yuw]	[ʊ]	[wʊ]
1. cool as a cucumber*	**6.** good books	**11.** I wouldn't care.
2. consumer reviews	**7.** sugar cookies	**12.** a tall woman
3. a booth for two	**8.** push or pull	**13.** a wool sweater
4. a dark blue suit	**9.** a good butcher	**14.** in the woods
5. future news	**10.** good-looking	**15.** a wild wolf

**cool as a cucumber:* calm in times of stress

2 HEARING DIFFERENCES

Listen to the words and repeat them. Then listen again and circle the word you hear.

1. a. Luke	**4. a.** wooed*	**7. a.** suit
b. look	**b.** wood/would	**b.** soot*
2. a. pool	**5. a.** stewed	**8. a.** shooed*
b. pull	**b.** stood	**b.** should
3. a. fool	**6. a.** who'd	**9. a.** cooed*
b. full	**b.** hood	**b.** could

**woo:* to win the affections of someone; *soot:* black dust left after burning; *shoo:* to make someone leave, to wave someone away; *coo:* the soft sound of doves or pigeons

3 ALTERNATING VOWELS

In some related words, the vowel alternates between [uw]/[yuw] and [ə]. The vowel in the more basic form is usually [uw].

A. Listen to the words and repeat them.

[uw]/[yuw]	[ə]
1. a. res**u**me	**b.** res**u**mption
2. a. cons**u**me	**b.** cons**u**mption
3. a. n**u**meral	**b.** n**u**mber
4. a. sed**u**ce	**b.** sed**u**ction
5. a. p**u**nitive	**b.** p**u**nish

B. With a partner, pronounce the pairs of words and decide whether the bold letters are alternating vowels or the same vowel. If they are alternating vowels, write "A" in the blank. If they are the same, write "S" in the blank.

1. st**u**pid—st**u**pefy S
2. ass**u**me—ass**u**mption ___
3. red**u**ce—red**u**ction ___
4. all**u**de—all**u**sion ___
5. st**u**dent—st**u**dy ___
6. m**u**tate—m**u**tant ___
7. imm**u**ne—imm**u**nity ___
8. prod**u**ce—prod**u**ction ___

4 Idioms and Expressions

A. Listen to the phrases in column A and repeat them. The bold vowels are [uw], [yuw], or [ʊ].

	A	B
___	1. l**oo**k up to (someone)	a. be in someone's sit**u**ation
___	2. l**o**se your shirt	b. **u**se infl**ue**nce to avoid r**u**les or regulations
___	3. be in someone's sh**oe**s	c. survive
___	4. p**u**t up with	d. tolerate
___	5. p**u**ll thr**ough**	e. admire or respect someone
___	6. p**u**ll strings	f. lose all your money
___	7. p**u**ll together	g. c**oo**perate, **u**nite during bad times

B. Match each phrase in column A with its meaning in column B. Compare your answers with a partner. Do you have the same answers?

C. Using the idioms from Part A, complete the dialogues. Then practice the dialogues with a partner.

1. A: I can't ____________ ____________ ____________ my r**oo**mmate any longer. She's just t**oo** p**u**shy. Can you help me get another r**oo**m?

B: In the middle of the semester? Well, maybe. I have a friend wh**o** works in the housing office. Maybe I c**ou**ld ____________ some ____________ for y**ou**.

2. A: I borrowed a lot of money to buy that stock. If the price keeps falling, I'm going to ____________ ____________ ____________.

B: Don't worry. You always buy risky stocks, and in the end, you d**o** all right. You'll ____________ ____________.

THE STRESS DIET

5 LISTENING: "The Stress Diet"

A. Listen to the recording and fill in the blanks.

Breakfast

1/2 ______
1 slice of dry wheat toast
1 cup of skim ________

Lunch

1 small leg of boiled chicken
1 ________ of spinach
1 cup of herb tea, with ________
1 small ________

________________ **Snack**

the rest of the ________ in the bag
2 cups of ice cream
1 jar of fudge ________
(for the ice cream)
nuts, cherries, whipped cream

Dinner

2 loaves of garlic ________
with cheese
a large pepperoni pizza
3 ________
________ cake with
thick frosting

Evening Snack

An ________ frozen
cheesecake, eaten directly
from the ________

B. Listen to the rules for the Stress Diet. Then answer the questions using the word *food.*

1. When don't calories count (the rules mention four cases)?
2. What effect do diet foods have on the foods they are eaten with?
3. How many calories do foods with the same color have?

C. In a small group, discuss the Stress Diet. Is it meant to be serious? Is there any truth in it? Share some examples of "stress eating" in your life.

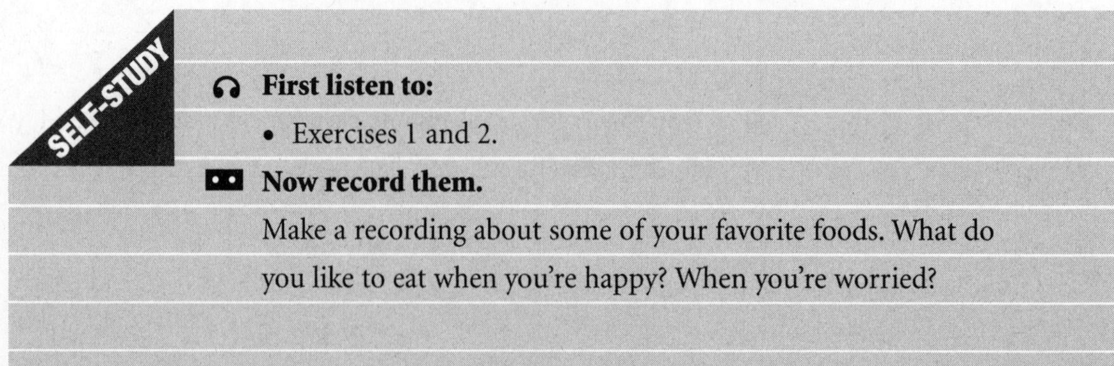

First listen to:

- Exercises 1 and 2.

Now record them.

Make a recording about some of your favorite foods. What do you like to eat when you're happy? When you're worried?

UNIT 10 [ay] wide, [aw] house, and [oy] boy Joining vowels together Alternating vowels: [ay] ~ [ɪ]

INTRODUCTION

The vowels in *wide, house,* and *boy* are complex vowels that end in [w] or [y]:

[ay] w**i**de [aw] h**ou**se [oy] b**oy**

These vowels are also called the "pain" vowels because English speakers use each vowel as an expression of pain:

Ay! Ow! [aw] Oy!

➤ JOINING VOWELS TOGETHER

When [ay], [aw], and [oy] are followed by another vowel, use [y] or [w] to join the vowels together. The vowels are in different syllables.

I ʸagree. sci ʸence now and then a boy and girl

➤ ALTERNATING VOWELS

In some pairs of related words, the stressed vowel alternates between [ay] and [ɪ]:

s**i**gn ~ s**i**gnal r**i**de ~ r**i**dden

➤ DIALECTS

Some Americans from the South pronounce [ay] like a long [ɑ]: *eye* sounds more like *ah*; *time* sounds more like *Tom.*

➤ TIP

Some students may need to pronounce the last sound of [ay] and [aw] more strongly, especially when the vowels are followed by [n] or [m], as in *time* or *count.* If this is a problem, concentrate on pronouncing the [y] of [ay] and the [w] of [aw] more strongly.

FOCUSED PRACTICE

1 PHRASES WITH COMPLEX VOWELS

A. Listen to the phrases and repeat them.

[ay]	[aw]	[oy]
1. a nice time	**5.** a town house	**9.** boys' toys
2. the right to privacy	**6.** a countdown	**10.** loyal employer
3. a bike ride	**7.** What about the drought?	**11.** spoiled boys
4. a tiny island	**8.** loud shouting	**12.** annoying noises

B. Work with a partner and take turns. Choose a phrase from Part A and say it to your partner. Pronounce the vowel carefully so your partner can tell you which word you said.

2 ALTERNATING VOWELS

In some related words, the stressed vowel alternates between [ay] and [ɪ]. The vowel in the more basic word is usually [ay].

A. Listen to the words and repeat them.

	[ay]	[ɪ]
1.	**a.** collide	**b.** collision
2.	**a.** decide	**b.** decision
3.	**a.** crime	**b.** criminal
4.	**a.** wise	**b.** wisdom
5.	**a.** cycle	**b.** cyclical
6.	**a.** hide	**b.** hidden

B. With a partner, pronounce the pairs of words and decide whether the bold letters are alternating vowels or the same vowel. If they are alternating vowels, write "A" in the blank. If they are the same, write "S" in the blank.

1. wide—width A	**6.** style—stylist ___
2. divide—division ___	**7.** wild—wilderness ___
3. guide—guidance ___	**8.** type—typical ___
4. excite—excitement ___	**9.** mild—mildness ___
5. divine—divinity ___	**10.** precise—precision ___

3 Joining Vowels Together

Listen to the sentences and words and repeat them. Then practice saying them with a partner. The underlined words in column A are joined together with [w] or [y]. They have the same or nearly the same pronunciation as the single word in column B.

	A	B
1.	Say "aunts."	séance*
2.	Is she going to sue it?	suet*?
3.	Did you dye it?	diet?
4.	Go in there?	Going there?
5.	Why are baskets sold here?	Wire
6.	I didn't like her sow* or chicken.	sour chicken

**séance:* a ritual to contact the dead; *suet:* hard animal fat used for cooking; *sow:* a female pig

4 The [ay]-[aw]-[oy] Game

Divide the class into two groups, A and B. Group A asks questions of Group B, and vice versa. All of the questions can be answered with common [ay, aw, oy] words or phrases. The team that is answering questions receives a point for each correct answer, correctly pronounced.

EXAMPLE

A: What do you call a male child?

B: *a boy*

Group A's questions are on page 246; Group B's questions are on page 252.

5 More Than Meets the Eye?

A. Is it possible to know something is going to happen before it happens? Can a mother feel when her child is in trouble? Take the quiz below to see whether you are a believer in extrasensory perception (ESP).

1. Have you ever gone to a psychic, fortune-teller, or palm reader to have your future predicted? If the answer is yes, was the prediction accurate? ______
2. Do you know anyone who has *premonitions,* strong feelings about future events that don't have a logical explanation? If so, have the premonitions ever come true? ______
3. Do you believe there are people with *precognition,* the power to predict the future? ______
4. Do you believe that some people have the power of *telepathy* and can "read minds"? ______
5. Do you believe in *psychokinesis,* the ability to make objects move with your mind? ______
6. Do you believe that some people are *clairvoyant,* able to "sense" or "see" distant events? ______
7. Have you ever had *déjà vu,* an inexplicable feeling that you have lived this exact moment before? ______

B. Compare your answers with two other students. Are you skeptics (doubters) of ESP or believers? Share stories you have about ESP.

6 Listening: *"ESP"*

A. Before you listen, read the questions. As you listen to the recording, write short answers. Listen to the recording again if you need to.

1. What percentage of Americans think that ESP exists?

____

2. What's the difference between a fortune-teller and a parapsychologist?

____

3. What are the three areas of ESP that have been studied the most?

____

4. What are Zener cards used for?

____

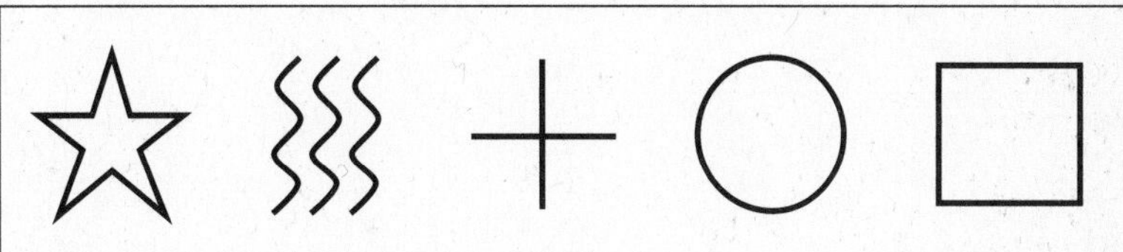

 **B. With a partner, conduct a classic telepathy experiment using the Zener card above. Read the instructions before you begin.**

- One student is the "sender" and the other is the "receiver."
- Sender: Hold your book on your lap so you are looking down at the Zener card and the receiver can't see your eyes. Look at one of the images and say "Now." Concentrate hard on the image for a few seconds, then say "Stop."
- Receiver: When the sender says "Now," try to read his/her thoughts and "see" the image in the sender's mind. When the sender says "Stop," point to the image you believe the sender was thinking of.
- Repeat the process ten times. Then, switch roles and do it again.

 **C. Report the results of your experiment to the class. Do any students have ESP? Can you think of other explanations for doing well in this experiment?**

First listen to:

- Exercises 1 and 3.

Now record them.

Make a recording about ESP. Do you believe in ESP? Why or why not? According to a national poll, half of Americans believe that some people have ESP. Why do you think so many people believe in ESP when most scientists are skeptical?

PART 2

CONSONANTS

UNIT 11 Consonant overview

INTRODUCTION

This unit presents an overview of the consonants: the vocal organs of the mouth used in making consonants; some consonants that are difficult for students; and the pronunciation of final consonants. Specific consonants and consonant contrasts are presented in more detail in subsequent units.

HOW CONSONANTS ARE MADE

Consonants are made by blocking the flow of air through the mouth. For example, when you say "P," your top and bottom lips press together, stopping the air briefly.

➤ THE MOUTH

Look at the diagram of the mouth. The labeled parts are the ones that English uses to make consonants.

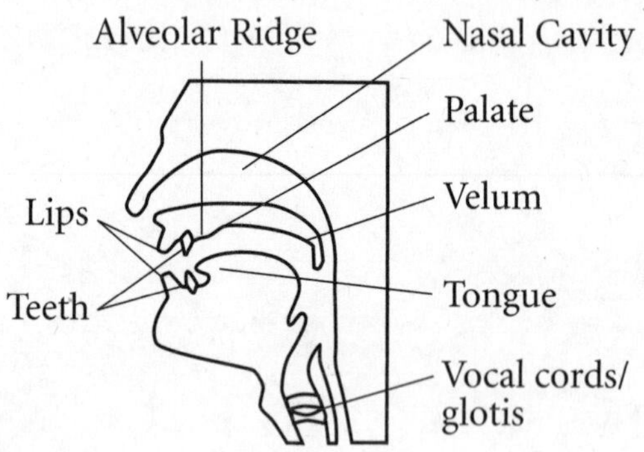

I FEELING SOUNDS

Work with a partner and do these mouth experiments.

A. Lips. Press your lips together and say "P." What other consonant sounds are made with the lips? Write words with these sounds on the line.

____

B. Teeth. Put the tip of your tongue between your teeth and say *thing.* Write some other words that begin with "th," and then practice saying them. Be sure to put the tip of your tongue between your teeth.

____

➤ AIR FLOW

The sound of a consonant also depends on how much the airflow is blocked. With a *stop* consonant, the air is completely blocked (or stopped) for a moment; with other consonants, there is less blockage.

2 FEELING SOUNDS

Work with a partner and do these mouth experiments.

A. Stops. The consonant [b] is a stop consonant. Put your mouth in position to say "B," but don't say it. Can you breathe through your mouth? Do the same thing with the other stops: P, T, D, K and the first sound in *go.*

B. Fricatives. Fricatives are "noisy" sounds, like [s] and [f]. They are produced when you partially block the air as it goes out the mouth. Make a long [sssssssss] and notice the "noisy" sound of [s]. The bold consonants in the words below are fricatives. Say the words slowly and listen to their noisy sound.

fine lo**v**e **th**ing ba**th** **s**ay ro**s**e **sh**oe wi**sh**

➤ VOICED AND VOICELESS SOUNDS

Consonants can be voiced or voiceless. When your vocal cords vibrate, the sound is "voiced," like the [z] in *zoo.* When your vocal cords do not vibrate, the sound is "voiceless," like the [s] in *Sue.*

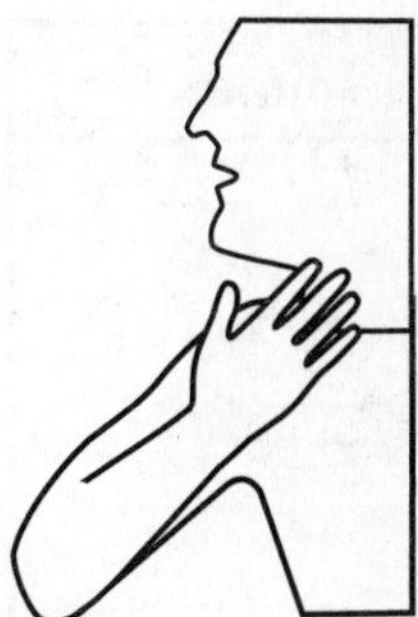

Try this experiment:

- Put your fingertips against the front side of your throat.
- Make a long [zzzzz] and feel the vibration in your fingers; [z] is a voiced sound.
- Make a long [sssss] sound. There is no vibration now because [s] is a voiceless sound.
- Alternate between [z] and [s] and feel the voicing turn on and off

[zzzssszzzssszzzsss].

3 Hearing Differences

A. Listen to the phrases and repeat them. Then listen again and circle the phrase you hear. The bold consonant in the first phrase is voiceless. In the second phrase, the bold consonant is voiced.

1. a. half a glass
   b. have a glass
2. a. an unusual H
   b. an unusual age
3. a. great prices
   b. great prizes
4. a. a new cup
   b. a new cub
5. a. a small lock
   b. a small log
6. a. The couple's wet.
   b. The couple's wed.

B. Work with a partner and take turns. Choose a phrase from Part A and say it to your partner. Pronounce the consonants carefully so your partner can tell you which phrase you said.

DIFFICULT CONSONANTS

Many students find these consonants difficult.

TH sounds	F and V	R	L
• Place the tip of your tongue lightly between your teeth.	• Gently touch your top teeth to your lower lip.	• Start with the tip of the tongue turned up and back a little. Lower the tongue tip without touching the top of the mouth.	• Touch the tip of the tongue behind the top teeth.

4 Fill in the Grid

Work with a partner. Each of you has a grid that is partially filled in with words. Student A has the words missing from Student B's grid, and Student B has the words missing from Student A's grid. Don't show your grid to your partner. Take turns asking each other for missing words. Pronounce the vowels in the words carefully. After you both complete your grids, compare them. They should be the same.

Student A's grid is on page 246. Student B's grid is on page 252.

CONSONANT CLUSTERS

Consonant clusters are groups of consonants. In English, they can occur at the beginning, in the middle, or at the end of words.

5 Hearing Consonant Clusters

A. Listen to the phrases and repeat them. Then listen again and circle the phrase you hear.

1.	**a.** black stairway	**b.** back stairway
2.	**a.** an expensive clone	**b.** an expensive cologne*
3.	**a.** please restrain it	**b.** please restain* it
4.	**a.** How many sports?	**b.** How many supports?
5.	**a.** They dried it.	**b.** They deride* it.
6.	**a.** a picture of water	**b.** a pitcher of water

**cologne:* type of perfume; *restain:* to stain (paint with a wood color) again; *deride:* to make fun of

B. Work with a partner and take turns. Choose a phrase from Part A and say it to your partner. Pronounce the consonants carefully so your partner can tell you which phrase you said.

FINAL CONSONANTS

In English, many words end in consonants. It is very important to pronounce final consonants, especially when they are grammatical endings: for example, the past tense of a verb or the plural of a noun. When final consonants are followed by another consonant, they are not pronounced strongly but they must be pronounced.

6 HEARING FINAL CONSONANTS

A. Listen to the phrases and repeat them.

1. **a.** a belt hanger — **b.** a bell hanger
2. **a.** six fish — **b.** sick fish
3. **a.** They attacked politicians. — **b.** They attack politicians.
4. **a.** build bridges — **b.** Bill Bridges
5. **a.** keep layers — **b.** key players
6. **a.** walked quickly — **b.** walk quickly

B. Listen to the recording and fill in the blanks with phrases from Part A.

1. Did you buy both a ______________ and a ______________?
2. Where are the ______________?
3. There are ______________ in the aquarium.
4. The pedestrians ______________.

C. Work with a partner. Take turns saying the sentence below, completing it with phrases from Part A. Pronounce final consonants correctly so your partner knows which phrase you said first.

Did you say "______________" or "______________"?

UNIT 12 Beginning and final consonants Joining final consonants Voicing of final consonants

INTRODUCTION

Beginning Voiceless Stops [p, t, k] **and Aspiration**

1. When [p, t, k] begin a word, pronounce them with aspiration, a strong puff of air (shown as "ʿ").

   pʿan   tʿan   cʿan

   Try this: Hold a piece of paper so the bottom edge is about 2 inches (5 centimeters) from your mouth.

   Say *pʿan*

   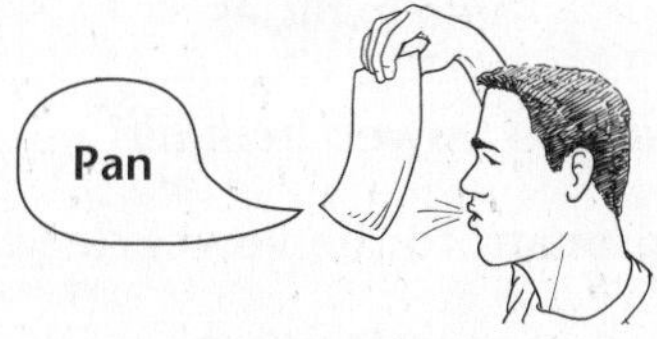

   Aspirate the [p]: The puff of air should blow the paper away from your mouth.

2. Aspirate voiceless stops when a stressed vowel follows.

Aspiration	apʿárt	attʿáck	decʿáy
No aspiration	ápple	áttic	décadent

Final consonants
Final consonants are pronounced more weakly than beginning consonants. The pronunciation of final consonants depends on the first sound of the next word. 1. Final consonant + different consonant: *stop sign* Pronounce the final consonant, but keep it short. Don't release (pronounce) it strongly (shown as ⁾). Don't add a vowel sound to separate the final and beginning consonants. stop⁾ sign   dot⁾ com
2. Final consonant + same consonant: *milk carton* Pronounce one long consonant (shown as "⁀")—don't say the consonant twice. black cat   bus stop Pronounce one long consonant when the two consonants are similar (for example, [f] and [v] or [k] and [g]). safe vehicles   egg carton
3. Final consonant + vowel: *fresh air* Join the consonant to the vowel clearly. atomic‿energy   keep‿it

FOCUSED PRACTICE

1 Aspiration

Listen to the phrases and repeat them. Aspirate the bold consonants.

1. **p**olitical **p**arties
2. a**p**ply for the **p**osition
3. su**p**port the **p**resident
4. re**t**urn the **t**ickets
5. **t**ake your **t**ime
6. **t**ell the **t**ruth
7. **c**ompact **c**ars
8. **c**rowded **c**lasses
9. a **q**uiet **c**ampus

2 Differences in Meaning

A. Listen to the phrases and repeat them. The bold final consonants in column A are not released strongly. In column B, the bold consonants are at the beginning of a word or syllable, so they are pronounced strongly.

Unreleased	Released
1. a. nigh**t** rate	**b.** ni**t**rate
2. a. shee**p** land	**b.** she **p**lanned
3. a. stoppe**d** racing	**b.** stop **t**racing
4. a. ma**k**e wrinkles	**b.** May **C**rinkles
5. a. migh**t** rain	**b.** my **t**rain
6. a. grea**t** rout*	**b.** gray **t**rout*

**great rout:* a military defeat (the army runs away); *trout:* a freshwater fish

B. Take turns reading sentences to your partner. Pronounce the bold consonants carefully so your partner can tell you what the sentence is about. Don't pause between the underlined words.

Sentence	The sentence is about:
1. a. Occasionally, the children stoppe**d** racing.	children racing
b. Occasionally, the children stop **t**racing.*	children tracing
2. a. There are for**k** racks on the table.	holders for forks
b. There are four **c**racks on the table.	damage to the table
3. a. Did he say, "Shee**p** Land Ahead?"	farmland
b. Did he say, "She **p**lanned ahead"?	advance planning
4. a. How much is the nigh**t** rate?	evening rates
b. How much is the ni**t**rate?	cost of chemicals

**tracing:* drawing by following a line

3 Hearing Long Consonants and Consonants Joined to Vowels

A. Listen to the phrases and repeat them. In column A, the underlined consonants are the same, so they are pronounced as one long consonant. In column B, the final consonant joins clearly to a following vowel.

One Long Consonant	Consonant + Vowel
1. a. like Coke	b. like oak*
2. a. white towel	b. white owl*
3. a. big Gabe	b. big Abe
4. a. both thighs*	b. both eyes
5. a. nice size	b. nice eyes

**oak:* a type of tree; *owl:* a large night bird with big eyes; *thigh:* the upper part of the leg

B. Work with a partner and take turns. Choose a phrase from Part A and say it to your partner. Join the words correctly so your partner can tell you which phrase you said.

C. Listen to the recording and fill in the blanks with phrases from Part A.

1. That dog has ______________ ______________ and is a ______________ ______________.

2. Did you say you ______________ ______________ or ______________ ______________?

3. ______________ ______________ told ______________ ______________ the news.

4. There's a ______________ ______________ near the ______________ ______________.

4 Final Voiced and Voiceless Consonants

In these pairs of words, the vowel in the first word is long because it is followed by a voiced consonant. The vowel in the second word is shorter because it is followed by a voiceless consonant.

A. **Listen to the pairs of words and repeat them.**

Long Vowel	Shorter Vowel
1. a. peas	**b.** peace
2. a. prove	**b.** proof
3. a. bags	**b.** backs
4. a. raised	**b.** raced
5. a. age	**b.** H
6. a. build	**b.** built

B. **Work with a partner. Take turns saying the sentence below, completing it with pairs of words from Part A. Pronounce the vowel and final consonant correctly so your partner knows which word you said first.**

Did you say "____________" or "____________"?

IT'S NOT EASY BEING GREEN

5 LISTENING: *"Hard Greens"*

"Hard greens" are environmentalists who propose unusual solutions to reduce man's harmful effects on the environment.

A. **Listen to the phrases and repeat them. Make sure you know what they mean.**

a footprint	output	dense cities
mainstream environmentalists	urban sprawl	fossil fuels
free range	livestock	growth hormones
wilderness		

B. **Read the questions and then listen to the recording. Listen again and answer the questions using complete sentences.**

1. What is the general solution proposed by hard greens to save the environment?

____

____

continued

2. Why do hard greens support the growth of large cities?

____

____

3. How do hard greens feel about the use of pesticides? Organic farming?

____

____

6 Making Inferences

With a partner, read the statements below and discuss them. If you think a hard green environmentalist would agree with a statement, write "hard green." If you think a mainstream environmentalist would agree with the statement, write "soft green." Write "both" if you think hard and soft greens would agree with it. Whi61ch statements do you agree with?

1. The government should provide financial incentives to high-rise developers and people who live in them. ____________
2. The government should increase subsidies on agricultural products to protect the small farmer. ____________
3. Growth hormones fed to milk cows should be banned. ____________
4. Nuclear energy plants should be closed. ____________
5. Safety regulations at nuclear energy plants should be stricter. ____________
6. National parks should prohibit snowmobiles because they disturb the wildlife. ____________

First listen to:

- Exercises 1 and 3A.

Now record them.

Then record your thoughts on these issues: How important is protecting the environment? Is the basic position of hard greens reasonable and/or practical? Why or why not?

UNIT 13 -*ed* endings Flapped [t] and [d]

INTRODUCTION

➤ PRONUNCIATION OF THE -*ed* ENDING

The -*ed* ending has three pronunciations, depending on the last sound of the verb.

Verbs ending in [t] or [d]			Verbs ending in a voiceless consonant			Verbs ending in a voiced consonant or vowel		
[əd] / [ɪd], a new syllable			[t], a consonant			[d], a consonant		
blend	blended	"blendəd"	promise	promised	"promist"	join	joined	"joind"
wait	waited	"waitəd"	walk	walked	"walkt"	stay	stayed	"stayd"

➤ ADJECTIVES ENDING IN -*ed*

The pronunciation of -*ed* adjectives follows the same rules as those for past tense endings.

an interested person   a matched pair   a bruised arm

However, in some adjectives, -*ed* is pronounced as the syllable [əd]/[ɪd], even though the base word doesn't end in [t] or [d]. Many of these adjectives end in [k] or [g]:

naked   two-legged   wretched

➤ ADVERBS ENDING IN -*edly*

In adverbs that end in -*edly*, -*ed* is usually pronounced as a separate syllable, [əd] or [ɪd].

supposedly   advisedly

➤ FLAPPED [t] AND [d]

When [t] and [d] are preceded by a stressed vowel and followed by another vowel, they are "flapped" or "tapped" (written [D]). The tip of the tongue hits the top of the mouth very fast. You can also think of this sound as a "fast D." The flap is a voiced sound. It is a characteristic feature of American English.

Listen to these words. The bold letters are flapped sounds.

le**tt**er   ri**d**er   wa**t**er   a**dd**ing   da**t**a   mi**dd**le

➤ FLAPPING AND HOMOPHONES

The flap creates *homophones,* words that are pronounced the same but spelled differently. Most speakers of American English pronounce these pairs of words the same:

latter—ladder   putting—pudding   liter—leader

➤ FLAPPING FINAL [t] OR [d]

Final [t] or [d] is often flapped in common words like *it, what,* or *at.*

Listen to these sentences. The bold letters are flapped sounds.

Pick **it** up.   Wha**t** are you doing?   He's **at** Ed's.

FOCUSED PRACTICE

1 PAST SENTENCES

Listen to the sentences and repeat them. Underline the syllables in the verb and write the number of syllables in the blank. Then check the pronunciation of the *-ed* ending.

	Syllables	[əd]/[ɪd]	[t]	[d]
1. The glass smashed on the floor.	1	___	✓	___
2. He invested in the railroad.	___	___	___	___
3. I offered to help.	___	___	___	___
4. The flight was delayed by the storm.	___	___	___	___
5. We finished the race last.	___	___	___	___
6. She persuaded me to do it.	___	___	___	___

2 Differences in Meaning

Work with a partner and take turns. Read either sentence *a* or sentence *b* to your partner. Pronounce the verb carefully so your partner can read the correct response to you.

Sentence	Response
1. a. These people paint pictures on walls.	graffiti artists
b. These people painted pictures on walls.	prehistoric cave dwellers
2. a. These people apply to medical schools.	people who want to become doctors
b. These people applied to medical schools.	doctors
3. a. They stop at Waterloo.	the Waterloo trains
b. They stopped at Waterloo.	Napoleon's army
4. a. These people cross the ocean to find gold.	multinational mining companies
b. These people crossed the ocean to find gold.	sixteenth-century Spaniards

3 Hearing Adjective Endings

Listen to the phrases and repeat them. The adjectives in the phrases end in *-ed.* As you listen, circle the adjectives in which *-ed* is pronounced as a new syllable ([əd] / [ɪd]).

1. all dressed up
2. a two-legged animal
3. an unanswered challenge
4. a changed man
5. my beloved wife
6. a shocked public
7. wicked policies
8. a wrecked car

4 FLAPPED [t] AND [d]

The bold sounds in the sentences are flaps ("fast Ds"). Listen to the sentences and repeat them. If the flap is hard for you to say, pronounce the sounds as [t] or [d].

1. Wha**t** are you doing?
2. Where's the wa**t**er me**t**er for the house?
3. I'd like a bi**t** of be**tt**er bu**tt**er.
4. What's the ma**tt**er with the la**dd**er?
5. They invited us to come a**t** eight.
6. Ge**tt**ing a man on the moon was a major accomplishment.

5 HEARING PAST TENSE VERBS

Listen to the sentences and write the missing verbs in the blanks. Then practice reading the sentences with a partner.

1. In October 1917, the Bolshevik Revolution in Russia ____________ in the establishment of the world's first communist state, the Soviet Union.
2. In 1991, elections ____________ the control of the Communist Party in the Soviet Union. The Soviet Union was dismantled and ____________ by several independent countries, with Russia as the largest and most powerful.
3. In 1962, scientists Watson, Crick, and Wilkins were ____________ the Nobel Prize for their discovery of the structure of DNA.
4. In the early 1900s, mass production of automobiles ____________ make the car an affordable part of everyday life.
5. In July 1969, Neil Armstrong ____________ out of the *Apollo 11* spacecraft and became the first man to walk on the moon.
6. In 1945, the atomic bomb was ____________ on Japan.

THE TWENTIETH CENTURY

6 LISTENING: *"The 1900s: Looking Back"*

At the turn of the twenty-first century, the World Book Encyclopedia invited experts in several fields to look back and list the ten most important developments of the twentieth century. Here are some of the developments that were suggested.

A. Read the developments and make sure you understand them. Then put a check in the "My Opinion" column next to the five developments you think are most important.

	My Opinion	Listening
1. use of the atomic bomb	___	___
2. World War II and theories on racial superiority	___	___
3. rise and fall of the Soviet Union	___	___
4. rise of nationalism	___	___
5. establishment of the United Nations	___	___
6. computers and the Internet	___	___
7. launch of *Sputnik I*	___	___
8. getting a man on the moon	___	___
9. development of antibiotics	___	___
10. machines to replace organ functions	___	___
11. discovery of the structure of DNA	___	___
12. advances in theoretical physics	___	___
13. civil rights movement	___	___
14. women's rights movement	___	___
15. widespread use of birth control	___	___
16. increase in world population	___	___
17. impact of the automobile	___	___
18. invention of the airplane	___	___

B. Before you listen, make sure you understand this vocabulary:

retrospective	supplement	kidneys	apartheid

C. Listen to the recording. As you listen, put a check in the "Listening" column for the developments that are mentioned. Compare your answers with a partner. Then discuss the developments that you and your partner think were most important. Would you add anything to this list? What developments of the twenty-first century so far will be remembered as important when this century closes?

First listen to:

- Exercise 1.

Now record it.

Then record your answers to these questions: In your opinion, what were the five most important developments or discoveries of the twentieth century? Why were they so important?

UNIT 14 "TH" sounds: think and these

INTRODUCTION

➤ THE CONSONANTS

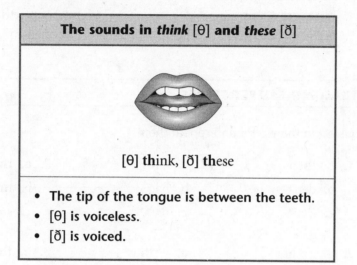

The sounds in *think* [θ] and *these* [ð]
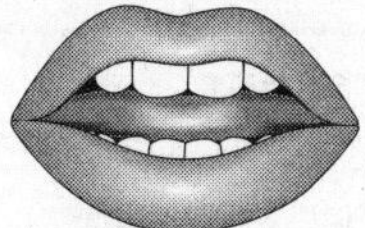 [θ] **th**ink, [ð] **th**ese
• The tip of the tongue is between the teeth. • [θ] is voiceless. • [ð] is voiced.

➤ SIMPLIFICATIONS OF *TH* SOUNDS

When words ending in *th* have an *-s* ending, the final *-th* is often dropped and the *-s* ending is lengthened: He breathes. (say, "He breazz" or "He breathes") the earth's resources (say, "the earsss resources" or "the earth's resources")
The plural *months* is almost always pronounced "mənts."
Clothes is almost always pronounced like the verb "to close."

FOCUSED PRACTICE

1 PHRASES WITH TH SOUNDS

Listen to the phrases and repeat them. Then practice them with a partner.

1. **th**irty-**th**ree **th**ousand
2. **th**ose **th**eaters
3. **th**reatening wea**th**er
4. bir**th** and dea**th**
5. Let's do some**th**ing toge**th**er.
6. mo**th**er and fa**th**er
7. **th**e fif**th** mon**th**
8. It's wor**th** a **th**ousand dollars.
9. my twentie**th** bir**th**day
10. a **th**oughtful au**th**or

2 HEARING DIFFERENCES

A. Listen to the words and repeat them.

1. a. **th**en
   b. den
   c. Zen*
2. a. au**th**or
   b. offer
   c. otter*
3. a. **th**ree
   b. tree
   c. free
4. a. ba**th**
   b. bat
   c. bass*
5. a. wri**th**e*
   b. rise
   c. ride
6. a. wi**th**
   b. wit*
   c. whiff*
7. a. **th**in
   b. tin
   c. sin
8. a. **th**inker
   b. sinker
   c. tinker*
9. a. soo**th**e*
   b. suit
   c. Sue's

**Zen:* a form of Buddhism; *otter:* a mammal like a seal; *bass:* a kind of fish; *writhe:* to twist and turn as in pain; *wit:* humor, intelligence; *whiff:* smell; *tinker:* make small attempts to repair something; *soothe:* calm

B. Work with a partner and take turns. Choose a word from Part A and say it to your partner. Pronounce the consonant carefully so your partner can tell you which word you said.

3 Sentences Full of Sounds

A. Listen to the sentences and repeat them.

1. Summer thunderstorms threaten the three thick but sick trees.
2. Someone should sing something soothing.
3. This theme seems thoroughly sorrowful.
4. Both boys were baffled* to see bass in the bathtub.
5. Either method is easier than those others.

**baffled*: confused

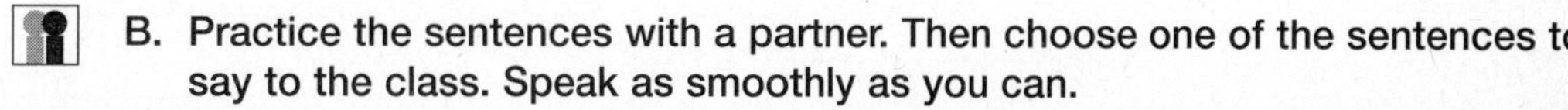

B. Practice the sentences with a partner. Then choose one of the sentences to say to the class. Speak as smoothly as you can.

4 The TH Game

Divide the class into two groups, A and B. Group A asks questions of Group B, and vice versa. All of the questions can be answered with a common TH word or phrase. The team that is answering questions receives a point for each correct answer, correctly pronounced.

EXAMPLE

A: What's 10 + 3?

B: *thirteen*

Group A's questions are on pages 246–247; Group B's questions are on pages 252–253.

5 Idioms and Expressions

A. Listen to these idioms and expressions and fill in the blanks. Compare your answers with a partner.

Idioms	Definition
1. ________ ________	in good times and bad times
and ________	to and from
2. back and ________	fail to happen, not happen
3. fall ________	It's obvious.
4. It goes ________ saying	find some good in a bad situation
5. make ________ most	mostly
of ________ situation	lose control (usually in anger)
6. on ________ whole	prefer
7. ________ a fit	
8. would ________	

B. Work with a partner. Choose idioms from Part A to complete the dialogues. Then practice the dialogues.

1. **A:** Suzy works too hard. She's always tired.

   B: Yes, but it's her own business, so she says she'll stay with it ________ ________ ________ ________.

2. **A:** When are you leaving for your vacation?

   B: Unfortunately, our plans have ________ ________, and we won't be going.

3. **A:** So you don't agree with the reorganization of the office?

   B: I wouldn't say that. ________ ________ ________ I think it's a good plan, but I think some of the details still need to be discussed.

OTHER THAN YOUR MOTHER TONGUE

6 Learning a Language

People learn languages in different ways. What works well for you? Read the statements and check whether you agree or disagree with them. Then discuss your answers in a small group. When giving your opinion, start with the phrase *I think that . . .* or *I don't think that . . . .*

	Agree	Not sure/ Sometimes	Disagree
1. Some people are just good language learners—it's easy for them to learn new languages.			
2. To learn new vocabulary, it's important to make lists and memorize new words.			
3. I don't consciously try to learn new words—I pick them up through the context.			
4. I like to learn through movies and television.			
5. I speak English a lot outside the class.			
6. I don't feel comfortable speaking because I make mistakes.			
7. I like to understand the grammar and have it explained.			
8. I like to play word games and do puzzles.			
9. The best way to learn a language is to live in a country where it's spoken.			
10. You need to study a language in a classroom in order to learn it.			

First listen to:

- Exercises 1 and 2.

Now record them.

Think about these questions, then record your answers: What's the hardest part of learning English for you? What sorts of things help you learn English? Television? Conversation with a native speaker? Reading books? Pronounce words with TH carefully.

UNIT 15 [p] pack, [b] back, [f] fan, [v] van, and [w] west

INTRODUCTION

➤ THE CONSONANTS

The sounds in *pack* and *back:* [p] and [b]	The sounds in *fan* and *van:* [f] and [v]	The sound in *west:* [w]
pack [p], **b**ack [b]	**f**an [f], **v**an [v]	**w**est [w]
• Press your lips together. • [p] is voiceless. • [b] is voiced.	• The top teeth gently touch the lower lip. • [f] is voiceless. • [v] is voiced.	• Beginning with [w]: Start with your lips tightly rounded and unround.

In formal speaking, words spelled with *wh* may be pronounced [hw]: *when, where, white, while.*

➤ TIPS

- If you have difficulty pronouncing the beginning [w] in words like *woman* and *wood,* start with your lips tightly rounded and unround a little. Or try saying two [u] sounds together: uuman (*woman*), uud (*wood*).
- Native speakers of Korean may confuse [p] and [f].
- Native speakers of Japanese should concentrate on [f] and [v].
- Native speakers of Spanish may confuse [b] and [v].
- Native speakers of German, Russian, Turkish, and Chinese may confuse [w] and [v].

FOCUSED PRACTICE

1 PHRASES WITH [p], [b], [f], [v], AND [w]

Listen to the phrases and repeat them.

1. in the first **p**lace
2. a **ph**one **b**ooth
3. **p**retty **b**ad
4. **b**ox o**ff**ice hits
5. a **v**ulnerable **p**erson
6. a so**f**t **v**oice
7. a cu**p** o**f** co**ff**ee
8. **W**hat **w**ould you do?
9. **v**ery **w**et **w**eather
10. on **p**ur**p**ose
11. a **f**unny **w**oman
12. an a**w**ful mo**v**ie

2 HEARING DIFFERENCES

Listen to the words and repeat them. Then listen again and circle the word you hear.

1. a. bury
   b. fairy
   c. wary
2. a. pet
   b. vet
   c. wet
3. a. pine
   b. vine
   c. wine
4. a. bite
   b. fight
   c. white
5. a. pale
   b. fail
   c. whale
6. a. aboard
   b. afford
   c. award

3 MOUTH SHAPES

A. Work with a partner and take turns. Choose one of the numbered sets in Exercise 2. Then face your partner and mouth (speak without sound) the words in the set in any order you want. Your partner must decide in which order you "said" the words by the shape of your mouth. Exaggerate the mouth position.

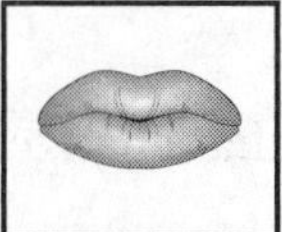

P or B

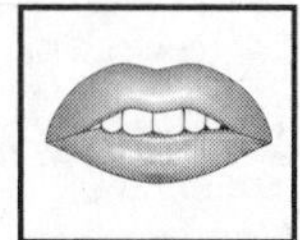

F or V

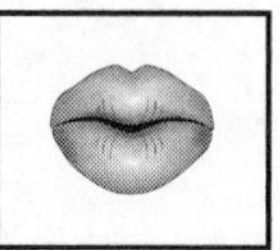

W

B. Now say a word from Exercise 2 out loud to your partner. Your partner will tell you which word you said.

4 DIALOGUES

A. Listen to the phrases and fill in the blanks. Compare your answers with a partner.

1. ____________ ____________ ____________
2. ____________ abuse
3. variable ____________
4. a ____________ ____________ flop
5. a ____________ physicist
6. ____________ ____________

B. Work with a partner and use the phrases from Part A to create short dialogues. Then practice the dialogues together. Be sure to pronounce P, B, F, V, and W correctly.

1. **A:** Who was Albert Einstein?
   B: ____

2. **A:** What's a term that means "hurting someone with words"?
   B: ____

3. **A:** How would you describe a "so-so" comedian?
   B: ____

4. **A:** What do you call a movie that people don't go to see?
   B: ____

5. **A:** What do Americans do every four years on the first Tuesday of November?
   B: ____

6. **A:** What do you call winds that change direction?
   B: ____

5 Box Office Hits

The *box office* is the area of a cinema where you buy your tickets. A *box office hit* is a movie that earns a lot of money. Box office earnings indicate a movie's popularity.

A. Work with a partner. Each of you has a chart that is partially filled in with the world's ten highest-grossing (moneymaking) movies (as of September 2002). The chart shows the title of the movie, the year it was made, and its box office earnings. Student A has the movies that are missing from Student B's chart, and vice versa. Don't show your chart to your partner. Take turns asking each other for the missing information. Speak clearly so your partner can write the information.

Student A's chart is on page 257. Student B's chart is on page 253.

B. As a class or in a small group, discuss the movies in the chart. Which movies have you seen? Which ones do you like? What are some movies released after September 2002 that have been very popular? Did you enjoy them?

First listen to:

- Exercises 1 and 2.

Now record them.

Record a description of one of your favorite movies.

Why do you like it?

UNIT 16 [s] sign, [z] zero, [ʃ] shop, and [ʒ] television

INTRODUCTION

➤ THE CONSONANTS

The sounds in *sign* [s] and *zero* [z]	The sounds in *shop* [ʃ] and *television* [ʒ]
sign [s], zero [z]	shop [ʃ], television [ʒ]
• Keep the tip of your tongue high and in the front of your mouth, behind the top teeth. • [s] is voiceless. • [z] is voiced.	• Pull the tip of your tongue back from the [s] position. • Round your lips a little. • [ʃ] is voiceless. • [ʒ] is voiced. [ʒ] is a rare sound in English. It does not occur at the beginning of words.

➤ SPELLING

The consonants [s], [z], [ʃ], and [ʒ] can be spelled in a variety of ways. Here are some spelling patterns as well as some exceptions that can cause confusion. See page 259 for a more complete list of spelling patterns.

1. *se* spellings	**[z] in most words:**	**nose, cause, these**
	[s] in some words:	**chase, house, release**
2. *ss* spellings	**[s] in most words:**	**kisses, passing, dress**
	[z] in a few words:	**scissors, possession**
3. *ssi* spellings	**[ʃ] in most words:**	**mission, Russian, session**
4. *ti(on)* spellings	**[ʃ] in most words:**	**nation, creation, inertia**
	[ʒ] in a few words:	**equation**
5. *si(on)* spellings	**[ʒ] in most words:**	**television, decision, collision**
	[ʃ] in a few words:	**dimension, expansion**

FOCUSED PRACTICE

1 PHRASES WITH [ʃ] AND [ʒ]

Listen to the phrases and repeat them.

[ʃ]	[ʒ]
1. I'm not **s**ure	**8.** on televi**s**ion
2. the Pacific O**c**ean	**9.** as u**s**ual
3. wa**sh**ing ma**ch**ine	**10.** lei**s**ure time
4. T-**sh**irts	**11.** mea**s**ure it
5. an elegant musta**che**	**12.** it's a plea**s**ure
6. I wi**sh** I could	**13.** on occa**s**ion
7. from **Ch**icago	**14.** a bei**ge** jacket

2 Hearing Differences

A. Listen to the words and repeat them. Then listen again and circle the word you hear.

1. a. raced	4. a. gashes*	7. a. assign
b. raised	b. gasses	b. a shine
2. a. cost	5. a. fierce	8. a. she'd
b. caused	b. fears	b. seed
3. a. bays	6. a. false	9. a. shoes
b. beige	b. falls	b. Sue's

**gash:* a long cut

B. Work with a partner and take turns. Choose a word from Part A and say it to your partner. Pronounce the consonants carefully so your partner can tell you which word you said.

3 Spelling and Sound

Listen to the words and repeat them. Decide whether the underlined sound is [s], [z], [ʃ], or [ʒ]. Then write each word under its corresponding column. Compare your answers with a partner. Do you have the same words in the columns?

1. dissolve	5. expansion	9. permission	13. purpose
2. classic	6. illusion	10. result	14. propose
3. nose	7. collision	11. casual	15. erase
4. dose	8. Asia	12. insure	16. glacier

[s]	[z]	[ʃ]	[ʒ]
	dissolve	5	7
2	3		6
8	4	9	11
13	12	12	14
	15		
16	10		

4 SENTENCES FULL OF SOUNDS

A. Listen to the sentences and repeat them. Group words together and pronounce the bold sounds carefully.

1. **S**ue **sh**ould per**s**uade the in**s**urance company to **s**weeten the deal before **sh**e in**s**ures her busine**ss** with them.
2. **Sh**e **s**ells **s**ea**sh**ells down by the **s**ea**sh**ore.
3. That **s**ign says "Sue'**s** **Sh**oe **Sh**ine **Sh**op," so I gue**ss** you can get your **sh**oes **sh**ined at Sue's.

B. Practice the sentences with a partner. Then choose one of the sentences to say to the class. Say the sentence as smoothly as you can and pronounce the bold sounds correctly.

LEISURE TIME

5 LISTENING: *"Leisure Time"*

A. Before you listen, make sure you understand this vocabulary:

sensual	spare time	quilt(ing)

B. Listen to the first part of the recording and fill in the blanks.

Why do people ____________ the ____________ ____________ they do? Not just for fun, says University of Florida psychologist Howard Tinsley. According to Tinsley's ____________, most hobbies and leisure activities fulfill a small number of needs: for example, the need for ____________, self-____________, or ____________ pleasure. "With so many people in jobs they don't care for, leisure is a ____________ aspect of people's lives," says Tinsley, "yet it's not something psychologists really study. Economists tell us how much money people spend on ____________, but nobody ____________ what it is about skiing that is really appealing to people."

C. The second part of the recording describes the needs that different leisure activities fulfill. As you listen, fill in what those needs are.

1. Acting and playing baseball ____________________
2. Fishing and quilting ____________________
3. Card playing ____________________

D. What are your three favorite leisure-time activities? What needs do you think they fulfill? Discuss your answers with a partner.

Activity	Need it fulfills
________	____________________
________	____________________
________	____________________

First listen to:

- Exercises 1 and 2.

Now record them.

Record a description of your favorite leisure activities. How much time do you spend a week on these activities? Why do you like doing them?

UNIT 17 [tʃ] check and [dʒ] judge

INTRODUCTION

➤ THE CONSONANTS

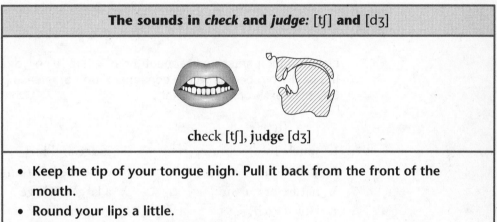

The sounds in *check* and *judge:* [tʃ] and [dʒ]
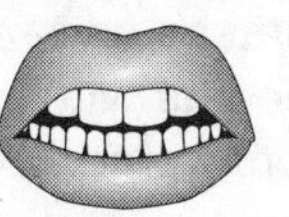 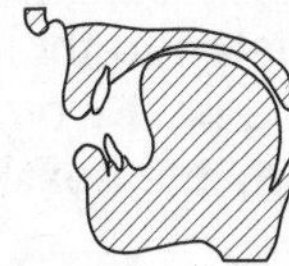 check [tʃ], judge [dʒ]
• Keep the tip of your tongue high. Pull it back from the front of the mouth. • Round your lips a little. • [tʃ] starts with [t]. It is voiceless. • [dʒ] starts with [d]. It is voiced.

➤ SPELLINGS

These sounds are sometimes spelled *tu* and *du.*

Spelling	Pronunciation	Examples
tu	[tʃ]	na**tu**re, fu**tu**re
du	[dʒ]	gra**du**al, e**du**cate

➤ TIPS

- If you pronounce *wa**tch*** like *wa**sh***, or *ma**j**or* like *mea**s**ure*, concentrate on pronouncing the [t] of [tʃ] and the [d] of [dʒ].
- If you pronounce *ca**tch*** like *ca**ts***, or *e**dge*** like *E**d's***, pull your tongue back and round your lips.

- If you pronounce *judge* like *judgy*, don't release the final sound so strongly. Keep it short.
- If you pronounce *edge* like *etch*, concentrate on making a voiced [d].
- If you pronounce *zero* like *dzero*, don't let your tongue make firm contact with the top of your mouth (doing this produces the [d] sound).

FOCUSED PRACTICE

1 PHRASES WITH [tʃ] AND [dʒ]

Listen to the phrases and repeat them. When [tʃ] or [dʒ] ends a word and the next word begins with a consonant, do not release [tʃ] or [dʒ] strongly. Say the next word immediately.

[tʃ]	[dʒ]
1. wa**tch** TV	7. **j**u**dge** and **j**ury
2. whi**ch** one	8. colle**ge** e**d**ucation
3. na**tu**re or nur**tu**re*	9. a lar**ge** packa**ge**
4. How mu**ch**?	10. gra**du**al chan**ge**s
5. in the fu**tu**re	11. gra**du**ate school
6. la**tch**key **ch**ildren*	12. **g**enetic en**g**ineering

**nature or nurture:* the debate over whether genetics ("nature") or the environment ("nurture") is more responsible for determining a person's character; *latchkey children:* children who come home to empty houses after school because their parents work

2 HEARING DIFFERENCES

A. Listen to the phrases and repeat them.

1. a. two pleasures	b. two pledgers*
2. a. Which witch?	b. Which wish?
3. a. cheap land	b. sheep land
4. a. no joking	b. no choking
5. a. cheering crowds	b. jeering* crowds
6. a. about the ridge*	b. about the rich

**pledgers:* people who pledge or promise to donate something; *jeering:* making fun of; *ridge:* the line of the top of a mountain

B. Work with a partner and take turns. Choose a phrase from Part A and say it to your partner. Pronounce the words carefully so your partner can tell you which phrase you said.

3 DIFFERENCES IN MEANING

Work with a partner and take turns. Read either sentence *a* or sentence *b* to your partner. Pronounce the underlined word carefully so your partner can read the correct response to you.

Sentence	Response
1. a. Why didn't you cash this?	They won't accept checks.
b. Why didn't you catch this?	I hurt my wrist.
2. a. They don't have mush* on the menu.	I'll have eggs then.
b. They don't have much on the menu.	Let's go somewhere else then.
3. a. Here's your share.	Are you sure you gave me half?
b. Here's your chair.	You did a nice job fixing the legs.
4. a. AIDS is an important health issue.	Research has still not found a cure.
b. Age is an important health issue.	We need more gerontologists.*

**mush:* hot, cooked cereal; *gerontologist:* doctor who cares for the elderly

EDUCATION CHECK

4 LISTENING: *"Educational Goals"*

In the United States, panels of experts are commissioned by the government periodically to examine the educational system.

A. Listen to the statements about the goals for public education in the United States and fill in the blanks. Then compare your answers with a partner. Did you hear the same words? Listen again if you need to.

1. Education ____________ not be about "getting ____________";
   it should be about discovering the ____________ of learning itself.
2. The goal of education is to keep the country in a strong, competitive ____________ ____________.
3. The goal of education is to improve the ____________ ability to ____________ a better ____________ and economic position.
4. The goal of education should be to build ____________ and understanding of other peoples and other ____________.
5. The goal of education is to produce socially responsible citizens, able to ____________ or become the ____________ leaders of the country.

B. Now listen to some of the problems facing public education. Take notes on each problem.

1. ____
   ____
2. ____
   ____
3. ____
   ____
4. ____
   ____
5. ____
   ____
6. ____
   ____

C. Work in small groups. Use your notes to summarize the problems mentioned in the recording. Then discuss these questions: Do you think the problems mentioned are specific to the United States, or do other countries face the same problems? What are some other problems? Think about your own education: Did you personally face any of these problems?

First listen to:

- Exercises 1 and 2.

Now record them.

Next, read this scenario:

In the United States, many decisions about education are made by local school boards. You are a member of a local school board with $1 million to spend this year on programs for children with special needs:

- children who need extra help with the basic skills of reading, writing, and math. Many have learning disabilities and need special classes.
- gifted children with above-normal intelligence. They are often bored in regular classes.
- children with special talent in music, dance, or art. Without professional training, their talents will not be developed.

The $1 million can help only two of these groups. Which group(s) will you vote to help and why? Talk for one minute about your decision.

UNIT 18 "S" endings

INTRODUCTION

"S" endings include the endings for regular plurals, possessives, third person singular present verbs, and contractions.

"S" endings have three pronunciations, depending on the last sound of the base word.

Words ending in [s, z, ʃ, ʒ, tʃ, dʒ] **(these are called "sibilant" sounds)**	**Words ending in voiceless sounds** [p, t, k, θ, f]	**Words ending in voiced sounds or vowels** [b, d, g, ð, v, l, r, m, n, ŋ]
[əz]/[ɪz] **(a syllable)**	[s] **(a consonant)**	[z] **(a consonant)**
one rose two roses	one ship two ships	one train two trains
Josh Josh's brother	I laugh. He laughs.	I play. She plays.

➤ NOUNS ENDING IN [f]

Several common nouns that end in [f] in their singular form end in [v] in the plural form. The plural ending is pronounced [z].

one leaf two leaves one knife two knives

➤ TH SOUNDS

TH sounds before "S" endings are often simplified or dropped.

one month two months [mənts]

FOCUSED PRACTICE

1 APPLY THE RULE

Write the plural ending for these nouns in the blank. Then put a check in the column for the correct pronunciation of the ending. Compare your answers with a partner.

	[əz]/[ɪz]	[s]	[z]
1. exercise s	✓	___	___
2. wife ___	___	___	___
3. ship ___	___	___	___
4. bush ___	___	___	___
5. bonus ___	___	___	___
6. conclusion ___	___	___	___
7. amount ___	___	___	___
8. salary ___	___	___	___
9. judge ___	___	___	___

2 HEARING SYLLABLES AND ENDINGS

A. Listen to the phrases and repeat them. Count the syllables in each phrase and write the number in the blank. Compare your answers with a partner.

1. a. some expert advice 5 — b. some experts advise 5
2. a. he claps ___ — b. he collapses ___
3. a. describe your folks ___ — b. describe your focus ___
4. a. Liz's Ford ___ — b. Liz Ford ___
5. a. quiet class ___ — b. quiet classes ___
6. a. good grades ___ — b. good grade ___
7. a. hard course ___ — b. hard courses ___
8. a. our hosts ___ — b. our hostess ___
9. a. fiscal condition ___ — b. physical conditions ___

B. Work with a partner and take turns. Choose one of the phrases from Part A and say it to your partner. Pronounce the words carefully so your partner can tell you which phrase you said.

3 IDIOMS AND EXPRESSIONS

Many idioms include verbs that describe physical exercise.

A. Listen to these idioms and expressions and fill in the blanks. Then compare your answers with a partner.

___ **1.** He wasted the whole day **running around in** ____________.

___ **2.** Stop **beating around the** ____________. Just say what you mean.

___ **3.** Get the ____________ first: **Don't jump to** ____________.

___ **4.** I've been sitting behind this desk for so long that I'm **climbing the** ____________. I've got to get out of the office!

___ **5.** I'm **bending over** ____________ to make you happy, but nothing I do ____________ you.

___ **6.** (at a casino) You've won $100 so far. Let's go home. Don't ____________ **your luck.**

___ **7.** Don't **pass the buck.** These ____________ are your responsibility.

___ **8.** You're **making** ____________ **out of molehills.** Who ____________ if she doesn't like your haircut?!

B. Work with a partner to match the idioms in Part A with the definitions below. Write the letter of the definition in the blanks next to the sentences in Part A.

a. avoid responsibility
b. take unnecessary risks
c. expend a lot of effort/energy without results
d. do everything possible to please someone
e. make a problem out of something that isn't a problem
f. want badly to be active, to take action
g. make decisions/judgments without enough information
h. speak indirectly

4 INTERVIEWS: *How much exercise do you get?*

Health professionals recommend that adults get about a half hour of moderate exercise four to five days a week to stay healthy.

A. Work with a partner. Interview your partner about exercise habits and write the information below.

Name ______________________

Do you like to exercise? ____________

How often do you exercise a week? ____________

What kinds of activities do you do and how much time do you spend doing them?

____

____

Do you think you get enough exercise? ______________________

B. Report the information from your interview to the class. Use present tense verbs and pronounce the "S" ending carefully.

First listen to:

- Exercise 2.

Now record them.

Then define these kinship (family) terms, using possessive nouns. Pronounce the "S" endings carefully.

uncle	paternal grandfather	stepson
niece	nephew	mother-in-law
granddaughter	aunt	brother-in-law

EXAMPLE

maternal grandmother:

Your mother's mother is your maternal grandmother.

UNIT 19 [y] yet and [dʒ] jet Joining vowels with [y] Clusters with [y] regular

INTRODUCTION

➤ THE CONSONANTS

The sound in *yet:* [y]	The sound in *jet:* [dʒ]
yet [y]	jet [dʒ]
• Raise the center of your tongue toward the front of your mouth. • The tip of your tongue rests behind your lower teeth.	• The tip of your tongue is high and pulled back to the center of your mouth. • Your lips are rounded a little. • [dʒ] starts with [d]. It is voiced.

➤ JOINING VOWELS WITH [y]

When vowels ending in [y] ([iy, ey, ay, oy]) are followed by another vowel, join the two vowels together with [y]. The two vowels are in different syllables. This happens when the vowels are in the same word or in adjacent words. (The letter "y" has been added to show the pronunciation.)

sci^y^ence   appreci^y^ate   my uncle   three^y^of those

➤ CONSONANT CLUSTERS WITH [y]

The sound [y] occurs in the consonant clusters of some common words. It is usually spelled with the letter *u.*

re**gu**lar [gy]   parti**cu**lar [ky]   po**pu**lar [py]

➤ SPELLING

[y] is the first sound of some words that begin with the letter *u*.

union **u**niversity **u**sually

➤ TIPS

- If you pronounce *yes* like *Jess*, try this: Say [i] and slide your tongue forward. Don't let your tongue press against the top of your mouth. Or say [i] twice: *iies (yes)*.
- If you pronounce *year* like *ear*, say [i] twice: *iiear (year)*.

FOCUSED PRACTICE

1 HEARING DIFFERENCES

A. Listen to the words and repeat them.

1. a. yellow
b. jello

2. a. year
b. ear

3. a. year
b. jeer*

4. a. yolk
b. joke

5. a. yet
b. jet

6. a. yeast*
b. east

7. a. mayor
b. major

8. a. the use
b. the juice

9. a. yes
b. Jess

**jeer:* to make fun of someone; *yeast:* bacteria that make bread rise

B. Work with a partner and take turns. Choose a word from Part A and say it to your partner. Pronounce the consonants carefully so your partner can tell you which word you said.

2 Sounds and Spellings

A. Fill in the blanks with *a* or *an.* Use *a* if the word begins with the consonant sound [y]. Use *an* if the word begins with a vowel sound. Join *an* and the next word.

1. He wore __an__ unusual hat.
2. She's a student at ___ university in Ohio.
3. There's going to be ___ union meeting tonight.
4. Take ___ umbrella—it's going to rain.
5. This is ___ unique opportunity to talk with an expert.
6. The book was about ___ utopian community in the future.

B. Compare your answers with a partner. Then practice saying the sentences to each other.

3 Sentences Full of Sounds

A. Listen to the sentences and repeat them. Group words together and speak smoothly.

1. Yes, Jess asked if the company's bought a new jet yet.
2. Last year my ear infections were bad.
3. Before he was a mayor, he was a major in the army.
4. Yellow jello tastes like lemon, doesn't it?
5. The scientists looked for younger animals in the jungle.

B. Practice the sentences with a partner. Then choose one of the sentences to say to the class. Say the sentence as smoothly as you can and pronounce the consonants correctly.

4 WORDS WITH [y] CLUSTERS

Listen to the phrases and repeat them. The bold letters are consonant clusters with [y].

1. ar**gu**ing style
2. parti**cu**lar uses
3. parti**cu**lar juices
4. re**gu**lar checkups
5. on a re**gu**lar basis
6. com**pu**ter users
7. po**pu**lar **mu**sic
8. **hu**man va**lu**es
9. a mi**lli**on years
10. voca**bu**lary books
11. am**bu**lance driver
12. se**ni**or year

5 JOINING VOWELS WITH [y]

A. Listen to these words. Are the underlined letters pronounced as two vowel sounds or as one? If there is only one vowel sound, write "1" in the blank. If there are two, write "2" in the blank.

1. appreciate 2
2. racial 1
3. immediately 2
4. official 1
5. experience 2
6. niece 1
7. worrying 2
8. denial 2
9. material 2
10. sufficient 1
11. theater 2
12. threaten 1
13. theory 2
14. theoretical 2
15. geography 2

B. Practice saying the words with a partner. If the letters are pronounced as two vowel sounds, join the two vowels with [y].

WHY ARGUE?

6 ARGUING STYLES

Arguments are a normal part of relationships. They can lead to growth or they can damage a relationship. Whether you argue with your father or fiance, your neighbor or nephew, your boss or best friend, you probably argue in a generally consistent way.

A. You and your partner each have eight questions about arguing styles. First answer the questions for yourself, and then take turns asking each other the questions. How similar are your arguing styles?

Student A's questions are on page 247; Student B's questions are on page 253.

B. **In this recording you will hear some advice about arguing effectively.* Listen to the recording and fill in the blanks. When you finish, go back to your answers to the questions in Part A. According to the advice, are you an effective arguer? Is your partner?**

1. Don't avoid ____________ at all costs. Bottled up __________ will find their way out in one ____________ ____________ another.
2. Don't argue in front of ____________ parties.
3. Bringing up old ____________ is a bad ____________. It's more ____________ to stay focused on one ____________.
4. Be a good ____________. Don't make quick ____________ about what your partner's "real" ____________ or feelings are.
5. At the end of an argument, make a ____________ offering. Tell your partner something you like about him or her.
6. Be ____________ to compromise but don't ____________ for things you haven't done or said.
7. Don't let an ____________ get out of ____________ and turn into a shouting ____________ where no one listens.

*Information from the Discovery Channel (Discovery Health.queendom.com, 2001)

First listen to:

- Exercises 1, 4, and 5.

Now record them.

Next, make a one-minute recording, answering these questions: Based on the advice from Exercise 6B and your answers to the questions in 6A, do you think you are an effective arguer? Why or why not?

UNIT 20 [r] rate Consonant clusters with [r] growth

INTRODUCTION

➤ THE CONSONANTS

The sound in *rate:* [r]	The sound in *late:* [l]
rate [r]	late [l]
• Turn the tip of your tongue up and back. • Then uncurl your tongue: Lower the tip of your tongue. • Do NOT let the tip of your tongue touch the top of your mouth as it uncurls. • Round your lips slightly.	• The tip of the tongue firmly touches behind the top teeth.

➤ CLUSTERS WITH [r]

The consonant [r] occurs in many consonant clusters. Don't separate the consonants in a cluster:

pray **tr**ain **thr**ee **shr**ink **scr**atch

➤ TIP

- If you pronounce *red* like "wed," make sure that you start with the tip of your tongue turned up and back. Then lower the tip of your tongue. If your [r] still has a *w* sound, don't round your lips at all—keep them flat.

FOCUSED PRACTICE

1 PHRASES WITH R

Listen to the phrases and repeat them.

1. rate of immigration
2. road trips
3. the wrong direction
4. increasing prices
5. transportation problems
6. roughly three-quarters
7. growth in urban areas
8. strict controls
9. foreign-born
10. permanent residents
11. historical trends
12. crowded areas

2 HEARING DIFFERENCES

A. Listen to the words and repeat them. Then listen again and circle the word you hear.

1. a. right
   b. light
2. a. arrive
   b. alive
3. a. crowd
   b. cloud
4. a. ride
   b. wide
5. a. present
   b. pleasant
6. a. correct
   b. collect
7. a. fright
   b. fight
8. a. prayed
   b. played
9. a. crash
   b. cash

B. Work with a partner and take turns. Choose a word from Part A and say it to your partner. Pronounce it carefully so your partner can tell you which word you said.

3 PHRASES WITH R AND L

Listen to the phrases and repeat them. Then practice saying the phrases with a partner.

1. parallel lines
2. religious problems
3. electric rates
4. friendly florist
5. really large salaries
6. celery and carrots
7. brilliant blue bracelet
8. a frightful flight
9. solitary celebrities
10. college library
11. allergic reactions
12. Florida alligators

4 Differences in Meaning

Work with a partner and take turns. Read either sentence *a* or sentence *b* to your partner. Pronounce the underlined word carefully so your partner can read the correct response to you.

Sentences	Responses
1. a. They erected bridges.	Over what river?
b. They elected Bridges.	To what office?
2. a. Don't step on that grass!	Did you just plant it?
b. Don't step on that glass!	Thanks. I might have cut myself.
3. a. Do you have the white books?	No, all my books are green.
b. Do you have the light books?	No, all my books are heavy.
c. Do you have the right books?	Yes, these are the right ones.
4. a. Do you like French flies?	No! I hate all insects.
b. Do you like French fries?	No, I'm allergic to potatoes.
5. a. There's a big cloud over there.	It looks like rain.
b. There's a big crowd over there.	I wonder what they're looking at.

5 Sentences Full of Sounds

A. Listen to the sentences and repeat them. Group words together and speak smoothly.

1. The children drew parallel lines representing railroad tracks.
2. Religious freedom is protected in the Bill of Rights.
3. Are your relatives really rock-and-roll celebrities?
4. Public loyalty to the royal family in Britain has a glorious tradition.

B. Practice the sentences with a partner. Then choose one of the sentences to say to the class.

6 Immigration Quiz

This is a quiz about immigration and the U.S. population. Each of you has three different questions. You also have sets of possible answers to your partner's questions. Here's how you play:

- Student A asks Student B three questions.
- For each question, Student B selects one of the possible answers. (Student A should give clues or extra information if needed about the correct and incorrect answers to help Student B.)
- When Student B has selected the correct answers, switch roles—Student B asks Student A three questions.

Student A's materials are on pages 247–248. Student B's materials are on pages 253–254.

7 Finding Reasons

A. Work with a partner and think of reasons people decide to live in another country.

Reasons why people immigrate (permanently or temporarily)

____

____

____

____

B. Share your answers with the class. Which reasons are the most common?

First listen to:

- Exercises 2 and 3.

Now record them.

Make a recording discussing some of the problems immigrants face when they come to a new country.

UNIT 21 Beginning [l] light Consonant clusters with [l] Contrasts: [l] and [r]

INTRODUCTION

➤ THE CONSONANTS

The sound in *light:* [l]	The sound in *right:* [r]	The sound in *night:* [n]
• Touch the tip of your tongue behind your top teeth. • When you say [l], there is contact between the tongue and the top of the mouth.	• Turn the tip of your tongue up and back. • Lower the tip of your tongue without touching the top of the mouth. • There is no contact between the tip of the tongue and the top of the mouth.	• The tip of the tongue touches behind the top teeth. • The air passes out through the nose, not through the mouth. Note: Some Chinese speakers confuse [n] and [l].

➤ CONSONANT CLUSTERS WITH [l]

Don't separate the consonants in the cluster.

Some beginning clusters: **cl**imb, **fl**y, **sl**ow, **spl**ash, su**ppl**y

Some final clusters: be**lt**, ho**ld**, mi**lk**, fau**lts**

FOCUSED PRACTICE

1 Phrases with [l]

A. Listen to the phrases and repeat them.

1. in love
2. love letters
3. a light lunch
4. a night-light
5. climb up
6. a large allowance
7. longer and longer
8. law and order
9. black clouds
10. clearance sale
11. It looks like rain.
12. eleven o'clock

2 Hearing Differences

A. Listen to the words and repeat them. Then listen again and circle the word you hear.

1. a. led
   b. red
   c. Ned
2. a. light
   b. right
   c. night
3. a. lot
   b. rot
   c. not/knot
4. a. collect
   b. correct
   c. connect
5. a. low
   b. row
   c. know/no
6. a. lock
   b. rock
   c. knock

B. Work with a partner and take turns. Choose a word from Part A and say it to your partner. Pronounce the consonants carefully so your partner can tell you which word you said.

3 Sentences Full of Sounds

A. Listen to the sentences and repeat them. Group words together and speak smoothly.

1. If you buy the right night-light, it will use very little electricity.
2. In your poem, be sure that all nine lines rhyme and have similar rhythm.
3. My connection to the Internet depends on the correction of a large collection of unrelated problems.
4. Late in the year the crime rate climbed a little.

B. Practice the sentences with a partner. Then choose one of the sentences to say to the class. Speak as smoothly as you can.

4 Consonant Clusters with [l]

Listen to the words and repeat them. Then practice the words with a partner. The first word in the pair starts with a consonant cluster. Do not separate the consonants. The second word starts with a consonant followed by an unstressed vowel.

1. a. claps
b. collapse

2. a. Pluto
b. polluted

3. a. blue
b. balloon

4. a. place
b. palatial*

5. a. inclusion
b. in collusion*

6. a. clone
b. cologne

7. a. glass
b. galactic*

8. a. slew*
b. salute

9. a. clam
b. calamity*

**palatial:* adjective for *palace; in collusion:* secret agreement to do something wrong; *galactic:* adjective for *galaxy; slew:* the past tense of *slay* (kill); *calamity:* disaster

REAL LOVE

5 Quotations

A. Listen to the quotes about love and fill in the blanks. The missing words have [r] or [l] consonants.

1. Love is the triumph of ____________ over ____________. (H. L. Mencken)
2. The ____________ wants what it wants. There's no ____________ to those things. (Woody Allen)
3. To say that you can love one person all your ____________ is just ____________ saying that one ____________ will continue burning as ____________ as you ____________. (Leo Tolstoy)
4. ____________ you need is ____________. (John Lennon and Paul McCartney, song title)

B. Work with a partner. Read these statements about love and then match the quotes in Part A with the statement below that expresses the same sentiment. Which quotes and statements do you agree with?

a. Love is not ruled by logic.
b. Love doesn't last.
c. Nothing is more important than love.

6 THE LOVE POLL

In 1999, Fox News Network conducted an opinion poll on love in honor of Valentine's Day.

A. Work with a partner. Each of you has half the questions from the poll. You also have the poll results, broken down by gender (whether the responses were from men or women). First, look at your own questions and answer them for yourself. Then ask your partner the same questions and record the responses. Do you agree?

Student A's questions and results are on page 248; Student B's are on page 254.

B. Write the class's answers to the poll questions on the board. How do they compare with the 1999 poll results?

First listen to:

- Exercises 1 and 2.

Now record them.

Think about the quotes in Exercise 5. Are they true for different kinds of love: romantic (between lovers), familial (among your family), philanthropic (love for humanity), platonic (between friends)? Talk for one minute about this subject.

UNIT 22

Final [l]: feel
Contractions of *will*

INTRODUCTION

➤ THE CONSONANT

Final [l] in *feel:* "Dark" l	**Beginning [l] in *leaf:* "Light" l**
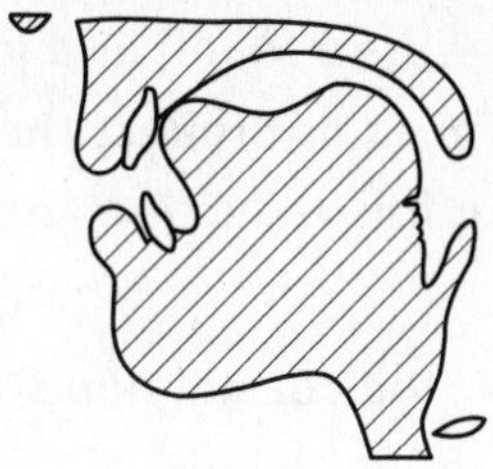 feel [l]	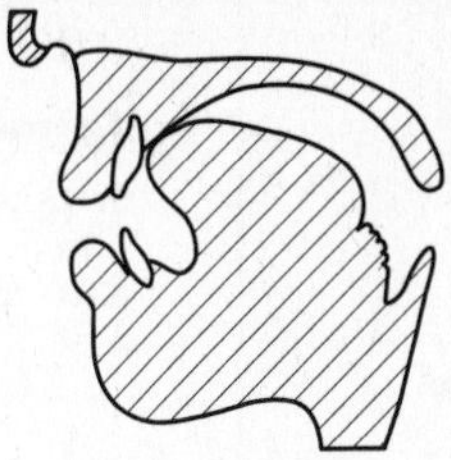 leaf [l]
• The tip of the tongue touches behind the top teeth. • The body of the tongue "bunches up" in the back of the mouth: The back of the tongue rises. • Final [l] has a "swallowed" sound: This pronunciation is called a "dark" [l].	• The tip of the tongue touches behind the top teeth. • The back of the tongue is not raised. • At the beginning of a word or syllable, [l] is called a "light" [l] or "clear" [l]. Most languages have a "light" [l].

➤ ENDINGS PRONOUNCED WITH DARK [l]: *-le, -al, -ful, -able, -ible, -ial*

little   local   capable

➤ CONTRACTIONS OF *WILL*

The contracted forms of *will* are pronounced with a dark [l]:

I'll go. He'll do it. You'll like her.

- **When *will* is contracted with a pronoun, the vowel of the pronoun is often reduced to a shorter sound:**

  I'll go. (say "all go")
  He'll stay. (say "hill stay")
  We'll go. (say "will go")
  You'll be late. (say "yʊll be late"; *you'll* rhymes with *pull*)
  She'll come. (say "shɪll come"; *she'll* rhymes with *still*)
  They'll do it. (say "thɛll do it"; *they'll* rhymes with *shell*)

- **After a noun, *will* is often reduced to [əl] and joined to the noun. The full form is usually written and does not reflect the reduced pronunciation. If it is difficult for you to make this reduction and join it to the noun, you can use *will* after nouns.**

  The coast will flood. (say "the coastal flood")

➤ SILENT "l"

The letter *l* is silent in many common words: *walk, talk, folk, half, would, could, should, chalk, palm, salmon, calm*

➤ TIP

- If you pronounce *old* like *ode,* or *people* like *peopo,* make sure that the tip of your tongue is firmly touching the top of your mouth.

FOCUSED PRACTICE

1 PHRASES WITH DARK L

Listen to the phrases and repeat them.

1. in the middle
2. single people
3. on the whole
4. double trouble
5. meanwhile
6. old people
7. in a little while
8. healthy children
9. logical results

2 ENDINGS WITH DARK L

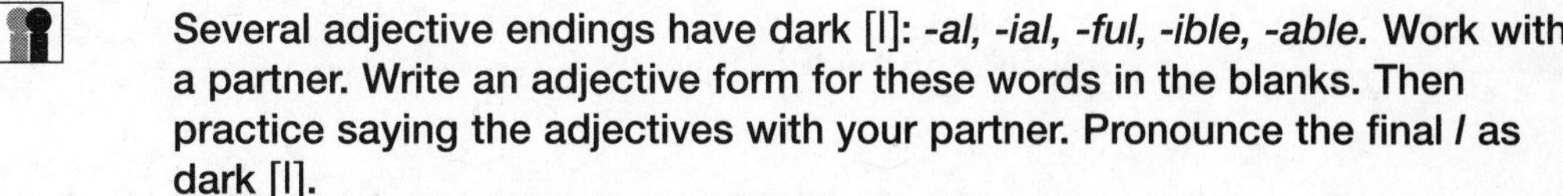

Several adjective endings have dark [l]: *-al, -ial, -ful, -ible, -able.* Work with a partner. Write an adjective form for these words in the blanks. Then practice saying the adjectives with your partner. Pronounce the final *l* as dark [l].

1. help ____________
2. believe ____________
3. president ____________
4. magic ____________
5. rest ____________
6. influence ____________
7. office ____________
8. reason ____________
9. finance ____________
10. harm ____________
11. sense ____________
12. compare ____________

3 REDUCTIONS OF *WILL*

Listen to the sentences and repeat them. Pronounce *will* as [əl] and join it to the noun before it. Practice saying the sentences with a partner.

1. What'll the future bring? (say "whaddəl")
2. I think a cure will be found for cancer. (say "curəl")
3. I think population growth will slow down. (say "growthəl")
4. His logic will convince you. (say "logicəl")
5. I think electric cars will replace gas-powered cars. (say "carzəl")
6. The earth will get warmer and the oceans will rise. (say "earthəl," "oceanzəl")

4 SOUNDS LIKE . . .

Two phrases that sound the same but have different spellings and meanings are called *homophrases.* Listen to these homophrases and repeat them. Then work with a partner to think of a homophrase with *will.* (You can check your answers on page 243.)

1. royal answer *Roy'll answer*.
2. the vinyl dye ________________
3. The cattle run away. ________________
4. your logical persuader ________________
5. Alaska fisherman ________________
6. the comical joke ________________

5 QUOTATIONS

Work in pairs for this exercise. Student A has clues to the missing words in Quotes 1 and 2, and Student B has clues for Quotes 3 and 4. Use the clues to help your partner figure out the words. Then practice reading the quotes out loud to each other. Most of the missing words contain dark l.

Quote 1: You can (a) ____________ (b) ____________ the (c) ____________ some of the (d) ____________, and some of the (e) ____________ (f) ____________ the time, but you cannot (g) ____________ (h) ____________ the (i) ____________ (j) ____________ of the time. (Abraham Lincoln)

Quote 2: That's one (a) ____________ step for (b) ____________, one giant (c) ____________ for mankind. ((d) ____________ Armstrong)

Quote 3: I have (a) ____________ you once, and I (b) ____________ (c) ____________ you again—your boys (d) ____________ not be sent into any (c) ____________ wars. (Franklin D. Roosevelt)

Quote 4: The (a) ____________ are (b) ____________ fond of new things. Young men read (c) ____________ but (d) ____________ men read newspapers. (G. K. Chesterton)

Student A's clues are on page 248; Student B's clues are on page 254.

WHAT WILL HAPPEN?

6 Predictions for the Twenty-First Century

A. Make predictions about what will happen in various areas in the twenty-first century. Use *will/won't* in your sentences.

1. Medicine/health ________________
2. Environment/the earth ________________
3. Technology ________________
4. Politics/government ________________
5. The family/relationships ________________
6. Transportation ________________
7. Other ________________

B. Work in small groups. Read your predictions to each other using *will* or the reduced pronunciation of *will.* Did you make similar predictions? Is your group optimistic or pessimistic about the future?

First listen to:

- Exercises 1 and 3.

Now record them.

What will your life be like in ten years? Will you be married? Will you have children? What will you do for a living? Where will you be living? Make a short recording discussing your predictions.

UNIT 23 [m] some, [n] sun, and [ŋ] sung Syllabic nasals: *sudden* Glottalized "t" and syllabic nasals: *cotton*

INTRODUCTION

➤ NASAL ("NOSE") CONSONANTS

The last sound in *some:* [m]	**The last sound in *sun:*** [n]	**The last sound in *sung:*** [ŋ]
some [m]	sun [n]	sung [ŋ]
• **Close your lips firmly.** • **The air passes out through your nose.**	• **The tip of your tongue touches behind your top teeth.** • **The air passes out through your nose.**	• **Raise the back of your tongue. The tip of your tongue rests at the bottom of your mouth.** • **The air passes out through your nose.**

➤ FINAL NASAL CONSONANTS

Nasal consonants are pronounced clearly at the ends of words. Do not drop them and "nasalize" the preceding vowel.

➤ PRONOUNCING [g] IN *ng* SPELLINGS

- **If *ng* ends the word, do not pronounce a [g] sound:**

  wro**ng** [ŋ] you**ng** [ŋ] bri**ng** [ŋ] sleepi**ng** [ŋ]

- **Pronounce [g] in the comparative and superlative of common adjectives that end in *-ng*.**

  long [ŋ] **longer** [ŋg] **longest** [ŋg]

- **Pronounce [g] in most words with *-ngle* spellings:**

  single [ŋg] **jungle** [ŋg] **tingle** [ŋg]

➤ SYLLABIC NASALS

In words like *cotton* and *given,* [n] is long and pronounced without a vowel. It is called a "syllabic nasal" (notation: [n̩]). Listen:

cotton [n̩] given [n̩] lesson [n̩]

➤ GLOTTAL SOUNDS AND SYLLABIC NASALS

A glottal stop ([ʔ]) is a quick closing of the vocal cords. It is the sound that separates the two parts of this warning word: *uh-oh* [ʔəʔow]. When [t] follows a stressed vowel and precedes a syllabic nasal, it is pronounced as a glottal stop [ʔ] (or a "glottalized t"). Listen:

co**tton** wri**tten** sen**ten**ce ea**ten**

➤ TIP

- If you have difficulty pronouncing [ŋ] by itself, without [g], concentrate on letting the air pass through your nose throughout the whole sound.

FOCUSED PRACTICE

1 Phrases with Final Nasals

Listen to the phrases and repeat them. Pay attention to final nasal consonants.

1. something's wrong
2. some time
3. wrong decision
4. someone else
5. mountain climbing
6. written down
7. I'm done
8. a long line
9. a long length
10. strong feelings
11. losing strength
12. young women

2 Hearing Sounds

Listen to the words and repeat them. If you hear a [g] sound, circle the word. Compare your answers with a partner and then practice saying the words to each other.

1. anger, hanger, angle
2. long, longer, longest
3. strong, stronger, strongest
4. springing, mingle,* stringy
5. single, finger, singer
6. tingle,* ringer, jingle*

**mingle:* mix; *tingle:* a stinging sensation, as from cold; *jingle:* a ringing sound, as from bells

3 Silent Letters

Listen to the words and repeat them. Look at the underlined letters and cross out the ones that are silent.

1. sign
2. signal
3. autumn
4. tongue
5. paradigm*
6. paradigmatic
7. columnar
8. column
9. angle
10. hanger
11. ringing
12. strongly
13. stronger
14. plumber
15. humble*

**paradigm:* an example that serves as a pattern or model; *humble:* modest, not proud

4 Jingle Bells

Many words that describe clear, musical sounds include [ŋ]. Fill in the blanks with words you hear to describe the sounds these things make.

1. Bells and phones ________________________________.
2. But small bells ________________________________.
3. Radar screens ________________________________.
4. And cold fingers ________________________________.
5. Stars ________________________________.
6. But water ________________________________.

5 Idioms and Expressions

A. Listen to the idioms in column A and repeat them. Pronounce the bold letters as syllabic nasals (long "n").

	A	B
c	1. writt**en** in the sand	a. dishonestly (as in money or power)
___	2. a hidd**en** agenda	b. I don't care at all.
___	3. hard-bitt**en**	c. temporary
___	4. writt**en** in stone	d. clean up
___	5. beat**en** up	e. a secret plan or purpose
___	6. ill-gott**en**	f. old and damaged
___	7. straight**en** up	g. unchangeable (a law, act, or decision)
___	8. I could**n**'t care less.	h. tough from experience (describing a person)

B. Work with a partner. Match the idioms and expressions in column A with the meanings in column B. Then practice saying the phrases to each other.

WANT TO SHARE?

6 LISTENING: *"Finding a Roommate"*

A. Listen to the recording and fill in the blanks. Then check your answers with a partner.

Finding a roommate can be ______________. And ______________ to share your ______________ space can be difficult. Lifestyle ______________ turn out to be the source of most roommate ______________. It's ______________ to find out as much as you can about a ______________ roommate so you don't make the ______________ ______________.

B. Fill out the Lifestyle Preference Form for yourself. Then check with other classmates to see whose answers best match your own. Do you think this person would make a good roommate?

LIFESTYLE PREFERENCE FORM

1. How would you feel if your roommate invited out-of-town visitors to stay overnight in your room/apartment?

a. I wouldn't like it at all.
b. It depends on the length of stay, how many visitors, etc.
c. I couldn't care less.

2. How often do you throw away uneaten food you've left in the refrigerator?

a. My food never makes it into the refrigerator—I eat it all.
b. About once a week.
c. Maybe once, when I move out.
d. Every day or two.

3. Where do you like to socialize?

a. I have a few close friends who come to my home from time to time.
b. I almost always go out when I socialize.
c. My door is always open—people are always coming and going.

4. How much TV do you watch?
   a. As much as I can.
   b. An hour or two a night.
   c. Two or three shows a week.
   d. I almost never watch TV.

5. What is your attitude toward money?
   a. I keep very careful track of my money—down to the penny.
   b. I sometimes forget to make payments and keep records.
   c. I'm pretty good at keeping track of what I owe and paying things on time.

6. How often do you straighten up your room?
   a. Always. I'm very neat.
   b. Every few days.
   c. Messes don't bother me, and I'm not a very neat person.

7. How do you feel when other people borrow your things?
   a. I don't care at all—everything I own is old and beaten up.
   b. I don't like to lend clothing or personal items, but I don't mind lending things like books or music.
   c. My things are my own, and I don't want anyone else to use them.

First listen to:

- Exercises 1 and 2.

Now record them.

Review your answers to the Lifestyle Preference Form in Exercise 6B. Then make a short recording, answering these questions: What type of person could you get along with easily? Have you ever had a roommate? Did you get along with your roommate?

UNIT 24

[h] heavy
Reductions of H-words

INTRODUCTION

➤ THE CONSONANT

The sound in *heavy:* [h]

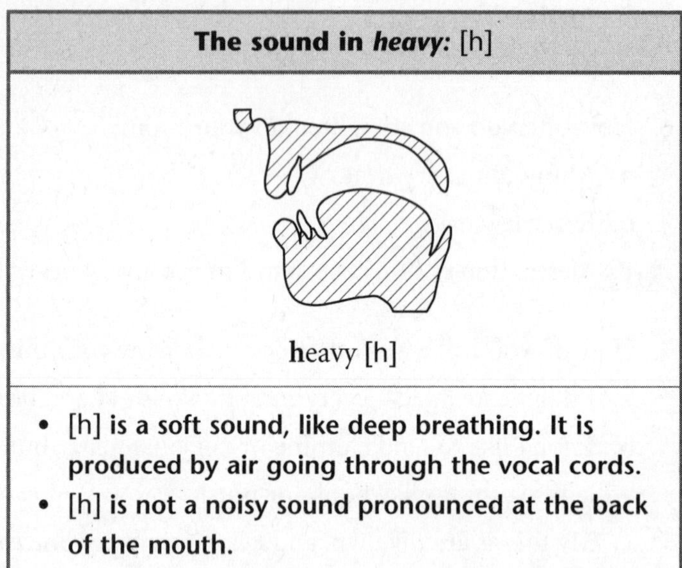

heavy [h]

- **[h] is a soft sound, like deep breathing. It is produced by air going through the vocal cords.**
- **[h] is not a noisy sound pronounced at the back of the mouth.**

➤ SPELLING AND PRONUNCIATION OF [h]

In some words the letter *h* is pronounced and in others it is not. These rules will help you know when to pronounce [h].

The *h* is never pronounced in some words. Most of these words came into English from French:

~~h~~our ~~h~~onor ~~h~~eir ~~h~~onest ve~~h~~ement ex~~h~~ibition

***H* is pronounced in most other words.**

heavy heart humorous however

***Wh* is pronounced [h] in these words:**

whole wholly who whom whose

➤ *H* IN PRONOUNS AND AUXILIARY VERBS

H may be pronounced or dropped in unstressed pronouns and auxiliary verbs (*he, him, his, her, have, has, had*).

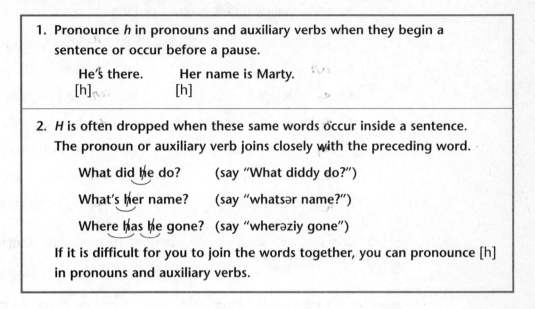

1. **Pronounce *h* in pronouns and auxiliary verbs when they begin a sentence or occur before a pause.**

   He's there. [h] **Her name is Marty.** [h]

2. ***H* is often dropped when these same words occur inside a sentence. The pronoun or auxiliary verb joins closely with the preceding word.**

   What did ~~h~~e do? (say "What diddy do?")

   What's ~~h~~er name? (say "whatsər name?")

   Where ~~h~~as ~~h~~e gone? (say "wherəziy gone")

   If it is difficult for you to join the words together, you can pronounce [h] in pronouns and auxiliary verbs.

FOCUSED PRACTICE

1 PHRASES WITH [h]

Listen to the phrases and repeat them. Pronounce [h] as a soft, breathy sound.

1. What happened?
2. a huge inheritance
3. Who is it?
4. a healthy heart
5. go ahead
6. a harmful habit
7. hot and humid
8. holding hands
9. a helpful hint

2 SILENT LETTERS

Listen to the words and repeat them. Cross out *h* when it is silent.

1. vehicle
2. vehicular
3. inhibit
4. inhibition
5. behind
6. behavior
7. dishonest
8. unhealthy
9. rehearsal
10. childhood
11. inherit
12. exhibit

3 HEARING [h]

A. Listen to the phrases and repeat them. Write the correct article in the blank. Write *a* if *h* is pronounced and *an* if *h* is silent. Then cross out *h* and underline the joining between *an* and the vowel following *h.*

1. an ~~h~~our ago
2. an herb garden
3. a holy site
4. a harmful substance
5. an honest mistake
6. a habitable area
7. a hospital bed
8. a heterogeneous population
9. a hero's welcome
10. an honorable agreement
11. a hazardous material
12. a wholesome meal
13. an heiress to a fortune
14. a high-risk occupation

B Compare your answers with a partner. Then practice reading the phrases with the correct article.

4 REDUCED [h] WORDS

Listen to the sentences and repeat them. The underlined words in each sentence are pronounced the same or nearly the same.

1. Would he ride with Woody Ride?
2. I bought him the present at the bottom of his list.
3. Don't wash her good dishes in the dishwasher.
4. Our church has asked for help from other churches.
5. I know she wants to practice boxing, but don't let her box the letter box.
6. Will he invite Willy?
7. Oliver Tripp paid for all of her trip.
8. The paint had dried on the half-painted wall.

5 GENETIC VERSUS ENVIRONMENTAL TRAITS

Some traits, like blood type, are inherited genetically. Others are learned from our environment and upbringing. However, scientists are not sure about many traits, especially those involving personality or style of thinking. These may be genetic or environmental or both.

A. Listen to these people talk about the ways in which they are like their parents. Write down each trait they mention.

G/L/B	Trait	G/L/B	Trait
_____	__________________	_____	__________________
_____	__________________	_____	__________________
_____	__________________	_____	__________________
_____	__________________	_____	__________________
_____	__________________	_____	__________________
_____	__________________	_____	__________________
_____	__________________	_____	__________________

B. Discuss the traits you heard with a partner. Are they inherited genetically, learned through upbringing, or perhaps both? For each trait, write *G* for genetic, *L* for learned, or *B* for both in the blank. Put a question mark (?) in the blank if you aren't sure.

First listen to:

- Exercises 1 and 2.

Now record them.

How much of who you are comes from your parents? Make a one-minute recording comparing yourself with your parents. Are you more like your father or your mother? Do you think these characteristics are genetic or come from your upbringing?

UNIT 25 Beginning consonant clusters

INTRODUCTION

Consonant clusters at the beginning of words and syllables may contain two or three consonants:

flight   stress   conflict   restrain

Some clusters with R and L:
brain   crash   flood   address   applaud
Some clusters with S:
stop   splash   spring   despite   square [skw]
Some clusters with W: The [w] sound is sometimes spelled *u*. The most common cluster, [kw], is usually spelled *qu*.
quiet   language [gw]   between   visual [ʒw]
Some clusters with Y: [y] is usually spelled *u* in clusters.
cute   regular   popular   vocabulary   onion
Rare clusters:
shrink [ʃr]   sphere [sf]   thwart [θw]

➤ PRONOUNCING CONSONANT CLUSTERS

Do not separate the consonants in a cluster with a vowel sound or add a vowel to the beginning of the word. It is important to pronounce the consonants as a cluster: Adding vowels could create a different word:

Consonant cluster	Separating the cluster with a vowel	Adding a vowel at the beginning
dress	duress	address
sport	support	a sport

FOCUSED PRACTICE

1 PHRASES WITH BEGINNING CONSONANT CLUSTERS

Listen to the phrases and repeat them. Be careful not to separate the consonants in the bold clusters.

1. **bl**ood **pr**essure
2. **chr**onic **pr**o**bl**ems
3. **tr**ibal **gr**oups
4. **cl**ear **thr**eat
5. **str**ess and **str**ain
6. **sn**ow**st**orm
7. esta**bl**ish **str**ategies
8. **sl**ow **st**eps
9. **tw**elve **qu**estions
10. collo**qu**ial lan**gu**age
11. po**pu**lar **vi**ews
12. re**gu**lar voca**bu**lary

2 HEARING DIFFERENCES

A. Listen to the words and repeat them. Underline the syllables. The words in column A begin with a consonant cluster. The words in column B begin with a consonant and vowel or with a vowel and consonant cluster.

	A	B		A	B
1.	sport	support	5.	strange	estrange*
2.	drive	derive	6.	clone	cologne
3.	steam	esteem	7.	sleep	asleep
4.	plight*	polite	8.	blow	below

**plight:* difficult situation; *estrange:* to make hostile, alienate

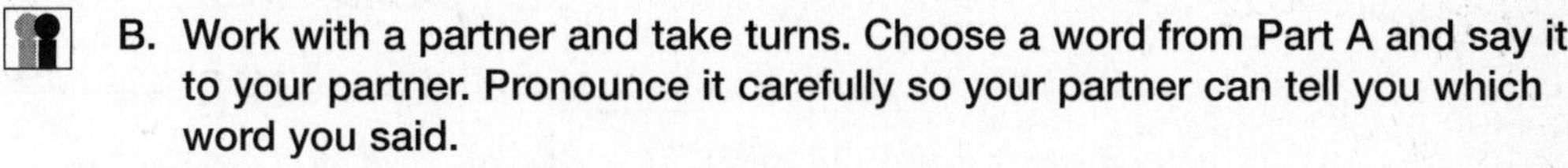

B. Work with a partner and take turns. Choose a word from Part A and say it to your partner. Pronounce it carefully so your partner can tell you which word you said.

3 SENTENCES FULL OF SOUNDS

A. Listen to the sentences and repeat them. Pronounce the consonant clusters carefully.

1. The steep stone steps lead from school straight to the stream.
2. I have no esteem for the state because its estate taxes are sky-high.
3. We prayed the parade would please the police.
4. The twelve twins screamed tricky questions across the quiet quadrangle.
5. We've got shrimp, flounder, crabs, clams, crawfish, lobster, squid, and trout.
6. Drive straight to the store without stopping and don't go astray.

B. Practice the sentences with a partner. Then choose one of the sentences to say to the class. Speak as smoothly as you can.

4 SPOONERISMS

"Spoonerisms" are mistakes that happen when the speaker accidentally switches the first sounds of two words. For example, *bone footh* is a spoonerism for *phone booth.* Consonant clusters are often involved in spoonerisms.

Work with a partner. In these spoonerisms the underlined words have switched beginning sounds. Decide what the speaker intended to say and write it in the blank. You may need to adjust spelling.

1. snovel the show *shovel the snow*
2. It crawls through the fax. ______
3. I was chipping the flannels on the TV. ______
4. our queer old dean ______
5. fighting a liar ______
6. a blushing crow ______
7. drain bamage ______
8. chilled grease ______
9. teepy slime ______

You can check your answers on page 243.

5 LISTENING: *"The Facts about Stress"*

Listen to the recording and fill in the blanks.

1. Acute stress is ____________-term. It is defined as the "fight or ____________" ____________ to an immediate ____________.
2. Ongoing ____________ situations ____________ ____________ ____________. The "fight or flight" response must be ____________.

6 STRESS STUDIES

Stress and its effects have been studied a great deal because they are so much a part of modern life. What do you know about the findings of these studies?

A. Read and discuss these statements with your partner. Write "T" in the blank for those you think are true, and "F" for those you think are false.

___ **1.** Adolescent boys and girls experience equal amounts of stress.

___ **2.** Stress is more likely to result in depression in boys than in girls.

___ **3.** These are both examples of situations that result in acute stress:
(a) narrowly escaping being hit by a car as you cross the street
(b) ongoing problems in your relationship with your spouse.

___ **4.** Persistent financial worries and pressure at work are examples of situations that cause chronic stress.

___ **5.** Virtually every system and organ in the human body is involved in the response to a stressful situation.

___ **6.** The effects of stress are always negative.

___ **7.** Educated individuals are more vulnerable to the effects of stress than less educated people.

___ **8.** Women are more vulnerable to the effects of stress than men.

You can check your answers on page 243.

B. We are all exposed to stressful situations. Some are short-term: for example, trying to get information from an automated answering system. Others are long-term: for example, caring for an elderly parent. Discuss with your partner situations that cause you short-term and chronic (long-term) stress and write them down. Talk about what you do to relieve the stress in your life.

Short-term stress	Chronic stress
______________________	______________________
______________________	______________________
______________________	______________________
______________________	______________________
______________________	______________________
______________________	______________________
______________________	______________________
______________________	______________________

First listen to:

- Exercises 1 and 2.

Now record them.

Make a short recording about a stressful situation in your life.

How did (do) you deal with it?

try at home!

UNIT 26 Final consonant clusters Joining final consonants

INTRODUCTION

Consonant clusters occur at the ends of many words and syllables in English. In general, final consonants are pronounced more weakly than consonants that begin a word or syllable—but they must be pronounced. When you speak, pay attention to the ends of words: Final consonants are an important part of clear, fluent speech.

work	belt	mix
[rk]	[lt]	[ks]

Grammatical endings can create large consonant clusters. Be sure that you pronounce grammatical endings: Grammatical endings are never dropped or simplified.

wor**ked**	be**lts**	mi**xed**
[rkt]	[lts]	[kst]

➤ JOINING FINAL CONSONANTS TO FOLLOWING WORDS

The pronunciation of final consonants depends on the sound that follows. Review these rules.

1. Final consonant + vowel: Join the final consonant clearly to the vowel.

worked out **ask a question**

2. Final consonant + same consonant: Pronounce one long consonant.

music class **help people** **both theaters**

3. Final consonant + different consonant: Don't release the final consonant strongly. Say the next word immediately.

black van **wives club** **he lives there**

FOCUSED PRACTICE

1 Joining Words Together

Listen to the phrases and repeat them.

Consonant + vowel

1. music awards
2. a heart attack
3. a hard article
4. scrambled eggs

Consonant + same consonant

5. big girl
6. help people
7. the fourth thing
8. hum music

Consonant + consonant

9. fast food
10. He takes charge.
11. We watched movies.
12. rap music

2 Hearing Differences

A. Listen to the phrases and repeat them. Then listen again and circle the word you hear.

1. **a.** lab broom **b.** lab room
2. **a.** talk fast **b.** talked fast
3. **a.** big eyes **b.** big guys
4. **a.** golf fan's course **b.** golf Ann's course
5. **a.** my contact's lenses **b.** my contact lenses
6. **a.** logged in **b.** log in
7. **a.** locked out **b.** logged out

B. Work with a partner and take turns. Choose a phrase from Part A and say it to your partner. Pronounce final consonants carefully so your partner can tell you which phrase you said.

C. Listen to the recording and fill in the blanks with phrases from Part A.

1. Did you say "__________ __________" or "__________ __________"?
2. I think I dropped __________ __________ __________.
3. I __________ __________ before I was __________ __________.
4. They __________ __________ on the phone.
5. In the painting, there's a girl with __________ __________ and __________ __________.

ELVIS PRESLEY

3 Apply the Rules

A. Listen to the phrases and repeat them. Using the notation symbols shown in the box, mark how the bold consonants are joined together. (*C* stands for consonant and *V* stands for vowel.)

1. C‿V	*box‿office*
2. C⁀C (same C)	*music⁀class*
3. C1 ' C2 (C1 and C2 are different.)	*hit ' music*

1. ro**ck st**ar
2. tale**nt sh**ows
3. acousti**c g**uitar
4. tru**ck dr**iver
5. Bea**le Str**eet
6. bla**ck bl**ues **m**usic
7. flamboya**nt cl**othes
8. we**nt w**ild
9. dignifie**d S**outher**n g**irls
10. pi**nk C**adillac
11. hi**t s**ongs
12. box offi**ce h**its
13. critica**l fl**ops
14. dru**g d**ependence
15. hea**rt f**ailure
16. devote**d f**ans

B. Compare your notations with a partner. Then practice saying the phrases.

4 Listening: *"Elvis Presley"*

Read the questions below and make sure you understand the words. Then listen to the recording about the life of Elvis Presley. Work with a partner to answer the questions using phrases from Exercise 3A.

1. Why is Elvis Presley famous?
2. Describe Elvis's interest in music when he was a boy.
3. What job did Elvis take when he graduated from high school?
4. What kind of music influenced Elvis?
5. During 1954 and 1955, Elvis went on tour through the South and Southwest. Describe the audiences' reactions to his live performances.
6. Describe Elvis's movies.
7. What kinds of problems did Elvis have later in his life?
8. How is Elvis still remembered by his fans?

5 Music

In small groups, discuss the kind of music associated with the artists listed in the box. Write the name of the artist(s) next to the type of music. What other artists can you think of? What other types of music? (You can check your answers on page 243.)

Yo Yo Ma	Enrique Iglesias	Bob Marley
Eminem	Louis Armstrong	Placido Domingo
Garth Brooks	The Beatles	Def Leppard

Type of music	Artists
1. Rap music	__________________
2. Country music	__________________
3. Latin pop	__________________
4. Heavy metal	__________________
5. Rock and roll	__________________
6. Jazz	__________________
7. Reggae	__________________
8. Opera	__________________
9. Classical	__________________
10. Other	__________________

First listen to:

- Exercises 1 and 2A.

Now record them.

Record answers to these questions: What kind(s) of music do you like? What kind(s) don't you like? Who are some of your favorite performers? When you answer the questions, pay attention to final consonants.

PART
3

SYLLABLES AND STRESS WITHIN WORDS

UNIT 27 Syllables and stress within words: overview

INTRODUCTION

This unit presents an overview of syllables and stress in words, including the characteristics of stressed and unstressed syllables and guidelines for predicting which syllable in a word is stressed. Specific topics are presented in more detail in subsequent units.

SYLLABLES AND STRESS

➤ SYLLABLES

Syllables are the "beats" of a word. The center of a syllable is usually a vowel, which can be preceded or followed by consonants. In the words below, the syllables are underlined. Use your finger to tap the beats (syllables) of these words:

face   approve   important   operation   organization

1 SYLLABLES

Work with a partner. Say the words, tapping the syllables with your finger. Underline the syllables and then write the number of syllables in the blank.

1. occur _2_	**5.** clothes ___	**9.** idea ___
2. match ___	**6.** society ___	**10.** negotiation ___
3. pleased ___	**7.** liked ___	**11.** artificial ___
4. management ___	**8.** surgeon ___	**12.** crash ___

➤ THE STRESSED SYLLABLE

One syllable in the word has primary or heavy stress. The vowel in that syllable is longer than vowels in other syllables. The stressed vowel may also be louder or pronounced on a higher pitch (note). You should focus on lengthening (holding) the stressed vowel.

2 STRESSED SYLLABLES

Listen to the words and put a stress mark (′) over the syllable with heavy stress. Then practice saying the words with a partner. Stretch a rubber band as you say the stressed vowel (or pretend to stretch one). This will help you lengthen the vowel.

1. photográphic	**4.** freedom	**7.** repeat	**10.** nationality
2. government	**5.** musical	**8.** tomato	**11.** historical
3. approval	**6.** disappointed	**9.** foundation	**12.** piano

➤ UNSTRESSED SYLLABLES

In English, unstressed syllables are reduced and short. The vowel is usually pronounced [ə] or [ɪ], regardless of how it is spelled. The alternation of long stressed syllables and reduced unstressed syllables is a key to natural-sounding English.

3 UNSTRESSED SYLLABLES

A. Listen to the words and repeat them. The words have been "respelled" by replacing unstressed vowel letters with their pronounced sound, [ə]. The line over the stressed vowel shows it is long.

1. əttrāctəv	**4.** pəlīcemən	**7.** Cānədə
attractive	________	________
2. rēasənəbəl	**5.** Āugəst	**8.** fāshənəbəl
________	________	________
3. məstāke	**6.** stətīstəcs	**9.** cəntēntəd
________	________	________

B. Practice saying the words with a partner. Then write the normal spelling of the word on the line. Notice that unstressed vowels can be spelled with any letter.

4 Hearing Differences

A. Listen to the pairs of words and repeat them. Notice that the stressed vowel helps you identify which word is being said. Mark the stressed syllable in each word with a stress mark (ʹ).

1. a. pérsonal — b. personnél
2. a. decade — b. decayed
3. a. desert — b. dessert
4. a. secret — b. secrete*
5. a. a rebel — b. to rebel
6. a. sever* — b. severe
7. a. despot* — b. despite
8. a. attic* — b. attack

**secrete:* to separate a substance from another by emitting it, to hide; *sever:* to cut; *despot:* tyrant, dictator; *attic:* space between the roof and ceiling

B. Work with a partner and take turns. Choose a word from Part A and say it to your partner. Exaggerate the stressed syllable so your partner can tell you which word you said.

5 Differences in Meaning

Work with a partner and take turns. Read either sentence *a* or sentence *b* to your partner. Pronounce the words carefully, lengthening the stressed syllable of the underlined word, so your partner can read the correct response to you.

Sentence	Response
1. a. What's the desert like?	It's hot, dry, and desolate.
b. What's the dessert like?	It's rich and chocolatey.
2. a. How do you spell "despot"?	D-E-S-P-O-T
b. How do you spell "despite"?	D-E-S-P-I-T-E

3. a. What are you going to do in the attack? — Defeat the enemy.

   b. What are you going to do in the attic? — Clean out some old boxes.

4. a. I need some personal information. — I'm single but I'm dating someone.

   b. I need some personnel information. — Here's a list of our employees.

➤ SECONDARY STRESS (ˋ) AND COMPOUND NOUNS

Some words have secondary stress in addition to primary or heavy stress. Vowels with secondary stress are not reduced to [ə]. They are shorter than vowels with primary stress and pronounced on a lower pitch. Compound nouns (noun + noun sequences) have primary stress and high pitch on the first noun, and secondary stress and low pitch on the second noun.

páss pòrt   áir lìne

6 PRIMARY AND SECONDARY STRESS

These words have both primary (ˊ) and secondary (ˋ) stress. Listen to the words and mark the stresses.

1. básebàll	4. hotel	7. Chinese
2. Web site	5. accent	8. password
3. makeup	6. postcards	9. outlive

SUFFIXES AND STRESS

When you learn a new word, you should always learn which syllable is stressed. When you add certain suffixes to words, you can predict which syllable will have primary stress.

Suffixes and stress
1. Stress the syllable in front of the suffixes *-ion, -ity, -ial, -graphy, -ic(al), -ious, -itude, -ian, -logy.* creátion creátivity artifícial biógraphy práctical
2. Stress the suffixes *-ee, -eer/ier, -ese.* engineér Japanése employeé
3. When most suffixes are added to a base word, the stressed syllable remains the same as in the base word: *-ness, -ment, -er/or, -(l)y, -able/ible, -ful.* góvernment (base word: góvern) réasonable (base word: réason) béautiful (base word: béauty) lóyalty (base word: lóyal)

7 Stress and Suffixes

Read the sentences and fill in the blanks with a form of the word in parentheses. Put a stress mark over the stressed syllable (′). Compare your answers with a partner. Did you mark the same syllables? Practice reading the sentences to each other, stressing the words correctly.

1. (identity, identify)

   The police could not ____________ the man with amnesia because he wasn't carrying any form of ____________. His ____________ was discovered only when his ____________ twin saw his picture on TV.

2. (politics)

   There are two main ____________ parties in the United States: the Democrats and the Republicans. ____________ who do not belong to one of these parties have little chance of being elected to a national office. However, third-party candidates can have an important influence on the ____________ of the major parties.

3. (real, realize)

   Rachel has always been a ____________ person with a clear view of ____________. The ____________ that her mother will not recover without a ____________ miracle has been ____________ hard on her.

UNIT 28 Primary and secondary stress Pronouncing unstressed syllables "Dropped" syllables Movable stress

INTRODUCTION

Syllables have one of three levels of stress: primary stress, secondary stress, or no stress (unstressed).

Level of stress	Vowel quality	Vowel length	Vowel loudness	Pitch
Primary stress: políte The stressed syllable is the most important syllable in the word.	Full vowel	Longest	Loudest	High
Secondary stress: áirplàne Written "\`" Secondary stress occurs • on the second noun of a compound: ráilròad • two syllables back from primary stress in some words: còrporátion ìnstitútion • on some suffixes: *-ize, -ate* (as a verb ending): apólogìze éducàte	Full vowel	Long	Loud	Low
Unstressed: ago	Reduced to [ə]/[ɪ]	Short	Not loud	Low

➤ PRONOUNCING UNSTRESSED SYLLABLES

Although unstressed syllables are not prominent, in most words they must be pronounced. Be especially careful to pronounce unstressed *y* endings, unstressed *er,* and unstressed *i* or *e* inside a word.

- Pronounce unstressed *y:* Did you say "the party" or "the part"?
- Pronounce unstressed *er:* Don't excise* the *er* of "exercise."
- Pronounce unstressed *i* and *e:* Say "evidence"—not "ev'dence."

**excise:* cut out

➤ DROPPED SYLLABLES

In some common words, unstressed syllables are dropped in speaking.

ev~~e~~ry (say "evry")   fam~~i~~ly (say "famly")   gen~~e~~ral (say "genral")

➤ MOVABLE STRESS

Primary and secondary stress sometimes "exchange" syllables in a word to create a more regular-sounding rhythm.

Movable stress in *-teen* numbers
• Stress *-teen* when a pause follows the number. This will make it easier for your listener to hear "nineteen" rather than "ninety." I'm nìnetéen. • Stress the first syllable of a *-teen* word when the next word begins with a stressed syllable (stress "moves back" to avoid two heavily stressed syllables in a row). 1999 (níneteen nínety níne)
Movable stress in words ending in a stressed syllable
• If the last syllable of a word has primary stress and a preceding syllable has secondary stress, the two stresses may change places to avoid two primary stresses in a row. She's Jàpanése.   but   She's a Jápanèse cítizen. *Jápanèse cítizen* has a more regular-sounding rhythm than *Jàpanése cítizen.*

FOCUSED PRACTICE

1 SECONDARY STRESS

A. Listen to the phrases and repeat them. Speak as smoothly as you can. In each pair of words, secondary stress occurs two syllables before primary stress. This creates a rhythmic alternation of full vowels (vowels with primary or secondary stress) and reduced vowels (unstressed).

1. scientific, economic: scientific and economic evidence
2. opportunity, creativity: an opportunity to show creativity
3. admiration, restoration: There's admiration for the restoration.
4. punctuality, reliability: We appreciate your punctuality and reliability.
5. engineer, volunteer: We need an engineer to volunteer.

B. Work with a partner. Take turns reading the words and sentences in Part A. Concentrate on a regular-sounding rhythm when you speak.

2 PRONOUNCING UNSTRESSED SYLLABLES

Listen to the words and repeat them. Join words together smoothly and make sure to pronounce all the syllables.

1. vigorous exercise
2. studying economics
3. very experienced
4. technological understanding
5. elemental energy
6. classical architecture
7. busy institutions
8. university article

3 HEARING SYLLABLES

A. One of the syllables in the words below is often dropped in spoken English. Listen to the words and draw a line through the unpronounced vowel.

1. int~~e~~resting
2. separate (adjective)
3. favorite
4. federal
5. miserable
6. different
7. practically
8. vegetable
9. general
10. evening

B. Listen to the phrases and repeat them. Count the syllables in each phrase and write the number in the blank. Then practice the phrases with a partner.

1. a. They separate parts. 5 b. the separate parts ___
2. a. a practical joke ___ b. practically a joke ___
3. a. carrying a lot ___ b. caring a lot ___
4. a. in the senator's office ___ b. in the center office ___
5. a. physical evidence ___ b. fiscal evidence ___
6. a. What's polio? ___ b. What's polo? ___
7. a. They're hungry in Poland. ___ b. They're Hungary and Poland. ___

4 Dialogues and Movable Stress

Work with a partner. Decide which syllable in the underlined words should be stressed to create the most regular rhythm (try to avoid two adjacent heavy stresses). Then practice the dialogues.

1. A: What does he like to do?
   B: Vòluntéer. He's a vòluntèer fíreman.

2. A: How much was it?
   B: Fourtéen.
   A: Exactly how much?
   B: Fourteen-fífty ($14.50).

3. A: What courses are you taking?
   B: Chìnése. And Chinese hístory.

CAREER COUNSELING

5 Occupations

A. Work with a partner. Listen to the words and repeat them. Then mark the stressed syllable in each word. Look up any words you don't know before continuing to Part B.

1. artículate	8. conservative	15. disciplined
2. uninhibited	9. responsible	16. ambitious
3. meticulous	10. persuasive	17. sensitive
4. creative	11. competitive	18. objective
5. logical	12. well-educated	19. curious
6. independent	13. imaginative	20. coordinated
7. extroverted	14. fearless	21. flexible

B In small groups, discuss what characteristics people in these lines of work should have and why. Use words from Part A and your own words.

Occupation	Characteristics
1. a politician	______________________
2. an actor	______________________
3. a scientist	______________________
4. a lawyer	______________________
5. an accountant	______________________
6. a reporter	______________________
7. a gymnast	______________________
8. a clown	______________________

C. In your opinion, what are the two most respected lines of work in Part B? The two most interesting? Which two do you think are the most highly paid? Share your answers with the class.

First listen to:

- Exercises 1 and 3A.

Now record them.

Choose two of the occupations from Exercise 5 and record a description of the characteristics someone in those occupations would need. Explain why the characteristics are important.

UNIT 29 Predicting stress: parts of speech and suffixes

INTRODUCTION

When you learn a new word, always learn which syllable is stressed. Here are some rules to help you predict the stressed syllable of some types of words.

➤ STRESS AND PARTS OF SPEECH

Two-syllable nouns: Stress the first syllable			
fúnction	ségment	clímate	
Two-syllable verbs and adjectives: Stress the "root" of the word (the part that carries the meaning, without prefixes or suffixes)			
First syllable is root:	óffer	públish	jéalous
Second syllable is root:	concéal	repéat	políte

➤ STRESS AND PREFIXES (SYLLABLES ADDED TO THE BEGINNING OF A WORD)

Short prefixes used to form verbs (*re-*, *dis-*, *in-*, *un-*, etc.): Do not stress the prefix, though the prefix may have secondary stress.		
remémber	disquálify	uncóver
Longer prefixes and prefixes that are also words (*inter-*, *over-*, *under-*, *out-*):		
• When used as nouns, stress the prefix.		
an óvercoat	an óutlaw	an ínterchange
• When used as verbs, stress the verb or root; the prefix has secondary stress.		
to òversée	to òutrún	to ìnteráct

➤ STRESS AND SUFFIXES (SYLLABLES ADDED TO THE END OF A WORD)

1. **Primary stress usually falls on these suffixes:** ***-eer, -ier, -ese, -ette, -esque, -ique, -ee*** **voluntéer   Chinése   cigarétte   uníque** **Exceptions:** ***-ee:*** **commíttee**
2. **Primary stress falls on the syllable in front of these suffixes:** ***-ial, -ual, -ian, -ion, -ient, -eous, -ious, -uous, -ic(s), -ical, -ity, -ify, -itive, -itude, -logy, -graphy*** **fináncial   politícian   creátion   relígious   publícity   áttitude** **Exceptions:** ***-ic:*** **Árabic, arίthmetic, pólitics** ***-ion:*** **télevision**
3. **Primary stress falls two syllables before these suffixes:** ***-ize, -ary, -ate*** **críticize   sécretary   vocábulary   óperate   délicate** **Exceptions:** ***-ize:*** **náturalize, cháracterize** ***-ary:*** **documéntary, eleméntary**
4. **Other suffixes and prefixes: When other suffixes and prefixes are added to words, the new word has the same stressed syllable as the basic word.** **háppy + ness   háppiness   púnish + ment   púnishment** **offícial + ly   offícially   góvern + or   góvernor** **advíse + able   advísable   proféssion + al   proféssional** **Exception:** ***-able:*** **cómparable**

TWO PRONUNCIATIONS OF THE SUFFIX *-ate*

1. **In verbs, pronounce** ***-ate*** **with secondary stress and a full vowel:** [eyt] **to dúplicàte** [eyt]
2. **In nouns or adjectives, reduce** ***-ate*** **to** [ət] **a dúplicate copy** [ət]

FOCUSED PRACTICE

1 STRESS WITH SUFFIXES

A. Listen to the words and repeat them.

-ion	*-ic(s)*	*-ical*	*-ious/eous/uous*
1. contribution	7. genetics	13. technological	19. superstitious
2. cooperation	8. problematic	14. physical	20. ambitious
3. imagination	9. scientific	15. cyclical	21. mysterious
________	________	________	________
________	________	________	________

-graphy	*-logy*	*-ian*	*-ity*
4. biography	10. biology	16. beautician	22. publicity
5. photography	11. astrology	17. physician	23. audacity
6. orthography	12. archeology	18. Indonesian	24. eccentricity
________	________	________	________
________	________	________	________

B. Work with a partner. Think of more words for each pattern and add them to the columns. Then read all the words in a column to your partner. Stress the syllable before the ending.

2 APPLY THE RULE

Work with a partner. Say the word in column A. Then mark primary stress on the words in column B (use the rules in the Introduction to help you). Can you add any related words to column B?

A	B
1. philosophy	philosopher, philosophical, philosophize
2. negotiate	negotiation, negotiable, negotiator, negotiability
3. apology	apologize, apologetic, apologetically
4. photograph	photography, photographic, photographer
5. profit	profiteer, profitable, profitability
6. compare	comparison, comparability, comparative
7. climate	acclimatize, climatology, climatic

3 DIALOGUES

Use words from Exercise 2 to answer the questions in the dialogues. Then practice the dialogues with a partner.

1. **A:** What do you call a person who takes photographs?
   B: photographer
   A: What courses should you take if you want to learn how to take photographs?
   B: photography

2. **B:** What do you do if you want to tell someone you're sorry?
   A: apologize
   B: How do you feel if you're sorry about something you've done?
   A: apologetic

3. **A:** When two nations disagree and don't want to go to war, what do they do?
   B: they negotiate
   A: If both sides agree to negotiate, how would you describe their demands?
   B: negotiable

4 WORDS ENDING IN *-ATE*

A. Listen to the words and repeat them. Remember that with nouns and adjectives, *-ate* is unstressed and reduced to [ət]. With verbs, *-ate* has secondary stress and is pronounced [eyt].

	Adjective/Noun	Verb
1.	**a.** graduate school	**b.** to graduate
2.	**a.** a duplicate copy	**b.** to duplicate
3.	**a.** an associate	**b.** to associate
4.	**a.** an estimate	**b.** to estimate
5.	**a.** climate	**b.** to acclimate*
6.	**a.** separate stories	**b.** to separate

**acclimate:* to become accustomed to a new environment

B. **Work with a partner. Decide how the underlined words are pronounced and practice reading the sentences to each other.**

1. His delicate health makes it hard for him to acclimate to extreme climates.
2. I can't estimate the cost of fixing the roof, so a carpenter is coming by today to give me an estimate.
3. I won't associate with your associates until they earn their certificates.
4. It's fortunate they can duplicate my duplicate copy.

ENGLISH 101

5 College Courses

A. **Listen to the words and repeat them. Then mark the stressed syllable. The words are taken from descriptions of college courses.**

1. genetics
2. laboratory
3. literary
4. comedic
5. conversion
6. document
7. allocation
8. mobility
9. autobiography

B. **Work with a partner. Each of you has a chart with information about the courses a student took during the fall semester. Student A has the information missing from Student B's chart, and vice versa. Don't show your chart to your partner. Take turns asking questions to complete your charts. Then discuss which courses sound most interesting to you.**

Student A's chart is on page 249. Student B's chart is on page 255.

First listen to:

- Exercise 1.

Now record it.

Discuss these professions, using the words in parentheses.

a. photographer (photographer, photograph, photography)

b. scholar (scholar, scholastic, scholarly)

c. politician (politician, politics, political)

UNIT 30 Compound nouns Stress in numbers

INTRODUCTION

Compound nouns are two nouns used together as one word:

railroad eyesight

➤ COMPOUND STRESS-PITCH PATTERN

The first word has primary stress and is pronounced on a high pitch. The second word has secondary stress and a lower pitch.

lánd scàpe 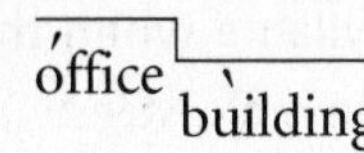 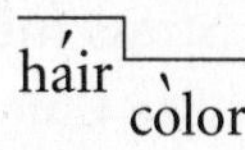

Use the compound stress-pitch pattern when two-word sequences that function as a unit are used as nouns.

- Adjective-noun sequences

  the Whíte Hòuse hárd wàre

  Sequences of adjectives and nouns which are not units have a different stress-pitch pattern.

  We live near the gréenhòuse. (an indoor area for plants; the noun is "greenhouse")

  We live near the gréen hóuse. (green color; the noun is "house")

  You can use the compound stress-pitch pattern in an adjective-noun sequence when the adjective is highlighted.

  A: Is your house the white one?

  B: No, I live in the gréen hòuse.

- Verb-preposition and preposition-verb sequences used as nouns

  máke ùp brúsh-òff óut gròwth óver sìght

➤ NUMBERS WITH *-ty* AND *-teen*

Numbers endings in *-ty*
Stress the number (the root): sı́xty   fı́fty The *t* in these numbers is pronounced as a flap (a "fast D"; see Unit 16): sixDy   fifDy
Numbers ending in *-teen*
Stress *-teen* when a pause follows the word: She's sixtéen. Stress the first syllable in the names of years: 1960: "nı́neteen sı́xty" Stress the first syllable when the next word begins with a stressed syllable (see Unit 28, "Movable stress"): She's 16. (sixtéen) *but* She lives at 16 Oak Street. (sı́xteen Óak Stréet)

FOCUSED PRACTICE

1 COMPOUNDS

Listen to the recording and fill in the blanks with the compounds you hear. Then practice saying the sentences with a partner. Use the correct stress-pitch pattern with the compounds.

1. The ____________ is so bright we don't need a ____________.
2. Don't forget to take a ____________ and ____________ on your trip.
3. I know the ____________ of your ________________________:
   He won't mind if you get another ____________.
4. I bought ____________, ____________, and ____________ at the ____________.
5. The ____________ for getting the announcement in the ____________ is tomorrow.
6. The baby started life in a ____________.
7. Who has records of your ____________ and ____________?

2 Differences in Meaning

Each phrase in the box has two meanings, depending on whether it is used as a compound or as two separate words. Read a question to your partner. Your partner should answer it with a phrase from the box pronounced with the correct stress-pitch pattern.

light + weights	black + board	green + house
checking + accounts	cheap + skates	dark + room

1. What do you call a house that's painted green?
2. What do you call the slate panel used in classrooms (you write on it with chalk)?
3. What do you call boxers weighing between 127 and 135 pounds?
4. How would you describe a pair of ice skates that didn't cost very much?
5. Describe the weights you should use when you first start weight lifting.
6. What do you call an indoor space used to grow plants?
7. What kinds of bank accounts allow you to write checks?
8. What kind of room does a photographer use to develop photographs?
9. Describe a flat piece of wood that has been painted black.
10. When an accountant is working for a client, what is he or she probably doing?
11. What do you call people who are stingy (who don't like to spend money)?
12. How would you describe a room that doesn't get much light?

3 Stress in Numbers

A. Listen to the recording and fill in the blanks.

1. It's an important birthday for her—she's _____.
2. Does the flight leave at _____ or _____?
3. This sweater is on sale for _________.
4. There are a lot of kids in my family and there's a big age range. I have a sister who's _____ and a brother who's _____.
5. My clock stopped at _________.
6. You didn't give me enough—I asked for _________.

B. Work with a partner and take turns. Read a sentence from Part A to your partner, using any *-teen* or *-ty* number. Use the correct stress-pitch pattern so your partner can tell you which number you said.

4 TRIVIA

Work with a partner and take turns. Each of you has five questions and answers taken from turn-of-the-century polls. You ask a question, and then your partner guesses the number (as a percentage of responses). Say "higher" or "lower" until your partner guesses the correct percentage. All of the answers are numbers that end in *-ty* or *-teen.*

Student A's questions and results are on page 249; Student B's are on page 255.

DESIGNER GENES

5 LISTENING: *"Designer Genes"*

A. Before you listen, make sure you understand this vocabulary:

test tube	lustrous	life span	bald	epilepsy

B. Read the traits given in the chart and then listen to the recording. You will hear a futuristic advertisement from a company that specializes in engineering perfect babies for prospective parents. Put a check next to the traits you hear mentioned on the tape.

Sex ___	Health
Appearance	Life span ___
Eye color ___	Heart disease ___
Hair color ___	Diabetes ___
Body type ___	Epilepsy ___
Skin color ___	Breast cancer ___
Height ___	Personality
Baldness ___	Outgoing ___
Abilities	Nonviolent ___
IQ ___	Addictive ___
Athletics ___	Friendly ___
Music ___	Hardworking ___
Art ___	Ambitious ___

C. In small groups, discuss genetic engineering. Do you think it would be a benefit to society? Why or why not? If genetic engineering were a reality, would you select any of your children's traits, or would you leave everything to chance?

First listen to:

- Exercise 1.

Now record it.

Record your thoughts on genetic engineering. Would you agree to altering an embryo's (fetus's) genetic makeup to correct health problems? To improve intelligence? To change appearance or personality?

UNIT 31 Words used as nouns or verbs Words with prepositional prefixes

INTRODUCTION

➤ WORDS USED AS NOUNS OR VERBS

Some two-syllable words are nouns when stressed on the first syllable and verbs when stressed on the second syllable.

Noun: They keep good récords. **Verb:** They recórd their expenses.

Here are some other words with this pattern:

addict	convert	increase*	produce	suspect
convict	insult	conflict	defect	project
refuse	contract	desert	permit	protest*
subject	contrast*	finance*	present	rebel

*Some speakers stress the first syllable of these words as nouns and verbs.

➤ WORDS WITH PREPOSITIONAL PREFIXES

These prefixes include *out-*, *over-*, *under-*, *up-*, *for(e)-*.

Verbs
The verb has primary stress; the prefix has secondary stress. **òutdó fòreseé òverloók ùnderstánd ùpstáge**
Nouns
The prefix has primary stress; the noun has secondary stress. **óversìght únderdòg óutràge úpstàrt**

FOCUSED PRACTICE

1 Stress Patterns for Nouns and Verbs

A. Listen to the words and repeat them.

	Noun	Verb
1.	a. cónduct	b. condúct
2.	a. rébel	b. rebél
3.	a. óbjèct	b. objéct
4.	a. prógrèss	b. progréss
5.	a. súspèct	b. suspéct
6.	a. prótèst	b. protést
7.	a. pródùce	b. prodúce
8.	a. pérmìt	b. permít
9.	a. óverflow	b. òverflów

B. Work with a partner and take turns. Choose a word from Part A and pronounce it as a noun or verb. Your partner will tell you which word you said.

2 Apply the Rule

Work with a partner. Fill in the blanks with the correct form of the word in parentheses and decide which syllable should receive heavy stress. Then practice reading the sentences to each other.

1. A learner's ____________ ____________ you to drive when there's a licensed driver in the car. (permit)
2. Although the police consider him a ____________, I ____________ he's innocent. (suspect)
3. A religious ____________ is someone who has ____________ from one religion to another. (convert)
4. The farm ____________ a wide variety of ____________. (produce)
5. There are ____________ opinions about the ____________. (conflict)
6. I ____________ to the large, ugly ____________ you've put there. Please move it. (object)

3 STRESS WITH NOUNS AND VERBS

Listen to the sentences and repeat them. Then practice saying the sentences with a partner; mark the stressed syllable of the underlined words.

1. You had the foresight to foresee the outrage we overlooked.
2. The overworked farmhands produced record amounts of produce.
3. There were conflicting reports about the conflict.
4. The researchers subjected the subject's forearms to a series of tests.
5. They say that forewarned is forearmed.
6. The soldier decided to desert in the desert.

4 PREPOSITIONAL PREFIXES

A. Listen to these words and make sure you understand them:

outcome	outrage	tortoise	underdog	uproar
foresee	outdistance	overjoyed	overtake	underrate

B. Listen to the recording and fill in the blanks.

The tortoise and the hare decided to race. The tortoise, of course, was the ______________. None of the forest creatures in the audience ______________ for a moment that the tortoise might ______________ the hare and win. But no one could ______________ the ______________ of the race. And, as we all know, the hare ______________ the tortoise.

When the race began, the hare easily ______________ the tortoise and was soon out of sight. But the tortoise ______________ to quit. With such a great lead, the hare ______________ himself to take a rest, which soon turned into a nap, and then, into a deep sleep. All the while, the tortoise was creeping along the course, making slow but steady ______________. Well, you know the story. The tortoise eventually ______________ the sleeping hare and won the race.

There was a joyous ___uproar___ from the forest animals during the minute or so it took the tortoise to cross the finish line. The entire audience was ___overjoyed___ to see the arrogant hare finally get his comeuppance.*

**comeuppance:* a deserved rebuke or penalty

KICK THE HABIT

5 Addictions or Habits?

A. What's the difference between an addiction and a habit? Listen to the dictionary definitions. Then, as a class or in small groups, discuss these excessive behaviors. Are they addictions, habits, or both? Are they dangerous? Here is some helpful vocabulary:

overdose	overeat	overdo	overwork	overwhelm	foresee
upshot	addict	conduct	produce	refuse	permit

Excessive behaviors

1. Gambling
2. Overeating
3. Drinking (alcohol)
4. Smoking (tobacco)
5. Taking illegal drugs
6. Taking prescription drugs
7. Vigorous exercise
8. Playing video games
9. Talking on the phone
10. Shopping
11. Working
12. Other ____________

First listen to:

- Exercise 3.

Now record it.

Choose two of the behaviors listed in Exercise 5 and make a brief recording about them. Why do you think people develop habits and addictions?

PART 4

RHYTHM

UNIT 32 Rhythm overview

INTRODUCTION

Rhythm is the patterning of strong (stressed) syllables and weak (unstressed) syllables in phrases and sentences. Rhythm also refers to the timing and grouping of words.

This unit provides an overview of some of the topics included as part of rhythm: stressed-timed languages, content and function words, and thought groups. Specific topics are presented in more detail in subsequent units.

STRESS-TIMED LANGUAGES AND SYLLABLE-TIMED LANGUAGES

English is a stress-timed language. This means that the time it takes to say a phrase or sentence depends on the number of stressed syllables, not on the total number of syllables. In syllable-timed languages like Spanish or Japanese, the length of time is determined by the number of syllables.

1 Spacing Stressed Syllables

Listen to the sets of sentences, and then practice them with a partner. Each sentence has the same number of stressed syllables but a different total number of syllables. The sentences in the set take about the same amount of time to say, and the stressed syllables are evenly spaced. Concentrate on making the stressed syllables long.

				Syllables	
				Stressed	**Total**
1. a.	TÚRN	RÍGHT	HÉRE.	3	3
b.	You should TÚRN	to the RÍGHT	at the LÍGHT.	3	9
c.	You should have TÚRNED	to the RÍGHT	at the LÍGHT.	3	10
2. a.	CÍties	NÉED	HÉLP.	3	4
b.	Our CÍties	will NÉED	our HÉLP.	3	7
c.	Our CÍties	will be NÉEding	our asSÍStance.	3	11

CONTENT AND FUNCTION WORDS

Content words are usually the stressed words in a sentence. Function words are unstressed.

Content words (stressed)	**Function words (unstressed)**
Nouns	Articles (*a, an, the*)
Verbs	Auxiliary verbs (*am/is/are/have,* etc.)
Adjectives	Personal pronouns (*I, you, him,* etc.)
Adverbs	Conjunctions (*and, or, when, if,* etc.)
Question words	Relative pronouns (*who, which, that*)
Demonstratives (*that, those*)	Prepositions (*to, at, in, on,* etc.)
Negatives, negative contractions	

2 DIALOGUES

Listen to the dialogues. Put a stress mark (ʹ) over the stressed syllable of content words. Then practice the dialogues with a partner. Space the stressed syllables as evenly as you can.

1. **Officer:** May I see your license?
   Stefan: What's the problem, Officer?
   Officer: Do you know you went through a red light at the intersection?
   Stefan: It was yellow—I'm sure it was still yellow when I crossed the intersection.

2. **Spokesperson:** Miss Ritter is going to make a statement at this time. She vigorously maintains her innocence.
   Miss Ritter: My arrest has been a big mistake. I was only pretending to be shoplifting. I'm preparing for a role in a movie—where I play a shoplifter.
   Spokesperson: Of course, she was going to return the merchandise. This has all been a big misunderstanding.

➤ REDUCTIONS OF FUNCTION WORDS

Many function words have two pronunciations: a "full," or word-list pronunciation, and a reduced pronunciation. The reduced pronunciation is used in speaking.

Reduced function words must be joined closely to the surrounding words. If it is difficult for you to join words together smoothly, you can use full pronunciations when you speak.

3 Reductions

Listen to the word in column A, and then listen to how it sounds in the phrase in column B. Can you hear the difference?

A Word list	B Normal reduced pronunciation
1. and	black and white (*black and white* sounds like "blacken white")
2. or	black or white (*black or white* sounds like "blacker white")
3. to	back to school (*back to school* sounds like "back tə school")
4. him	call him (*call him* sounds like "callim")
5. have	could have gone (*could have gone* sounds like "couldəv gone")
6. can	Your cooking can tempt* anyone. (*can tempt* sounds like "contempt")
7. he	Did he go? (*Did he go?* sounds like "Diddy go?")

**tempt:* be attractive, make someone want to do something

4 Hearing Reductions

Listen to the sentences and repeat them. The pairs of underlined words have the same or nearly the same pronunciation. Then practice the sentences with a partner.

1. He's fallen behind this fall and winter.
2. A noise annoys an oyster.
3. Bea can light the beacon light.
4. The winners have passed the winners of past years.
5. You can pick it up near the house with the picket fence.
6. I don't know how much fun he had in his funny hat.
7. My son's going to day school today.
8. The fortunate old woman made a fortune at bingo.

THOUGHT GROUPS AND BREATH GROUPS

Thought groups are meaningful phrases within a sentence. The words in a thought group are pronounced together, as a unit. Thought groups help the listener identify the parts of a sentence.

I'm leaving in the morning.

➤ GROUPING WORDS

There are no fixed rules for deciding which words to include in a thought group. Usually, meaning and sentence length determine which words belong together. Look at two ways to group the words in the sentence below.

We're going to stay at a hotel in Miami.

We're going to stay at a hotel in Miami.

➤ JOINING THOUGHT GROUPS

Join thought groups together by briefly holding the end of one thought group before saying the next. There may also be a small rise or fall in pitch between thought groups.

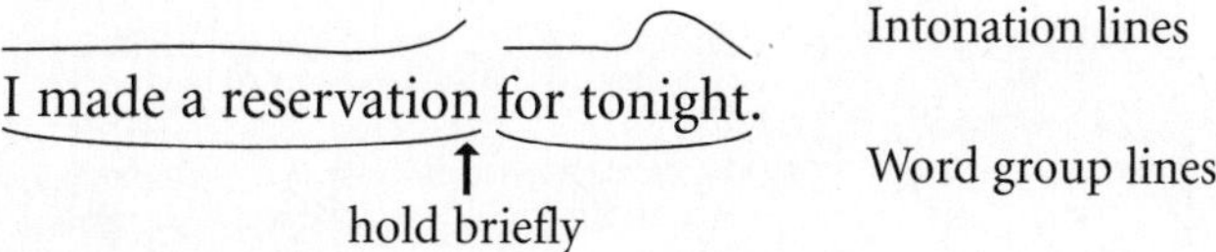

➤ BREATH GROUPS

Thought groups are combined into breath groups: words spoken in one breath. Breath groups are usually marked by punctuation.

5 THOUGHT GROUPS

Listen to the sentences and underline thought groups. Then practice the sentences with a partner.

1. Last summer, we decided to drive across the country.
2. We started in New York and planned to take the northern route, all the way to Seattle.
3. Coming from the east, the Rockies were spectacular.
4. They rose like a wall from the flat plains, running north and south as far as the eye could see.

6 LISTENING

A. Before you listen, make sure you understand this vocabulary:

monument	massive	pillars	fortress	Andes Mountains
Incans	terraces	steep	slopes	tombs

B. Listen to the recording. Then use the information to connect the phrases in the three columns and make sentences describing the places in column A.

A	B	C
Stonehenge	runs east and west	in the Peruvian Andes.
Machu Picchu	served as tombs	built of massive stone pillars.
The Great Wall of China	is a prehistoric monument	for kings and queens.
The pyramids of Egypt	was an Incan city	through northern China.

C. Work with a partner and take turns. Read the sentences that you created in Part B, pronouncing the three phrases as thought groups.

UNIT 33 Stressed and unstressed words Stress patterns

INTRODUCTION

Just as stressed and unstressed syllables make up words, stressed and unstressed words make up phrases and sentences. The patterning of stressed and unstressed words is an important part of English rhythm.

Words in a sentence are either content words or function words. Content words are usually stressed. They include words with clear meaning, like *computer* or *freedom.* Function words are unstressed. They are words that have grammatical meaning, like *to* or *an.*

Content words (stressed)

Nouns	*computer*
Verbs	*walked*
Adjectives	*intelligent*
Adverbs	*quickly*
Demonstrative pronouns and adjectives	*this*
Interrogative (*wh*) words	*Who? Why? Where?*
Negatives	*not doesn't*

Function words (unstressed)

Articles	*a, an, the*
Short prepositions	*to, at, in, on,* etc.
Conjunctions	*and, or, if, that,* etc.
Auxiliary verbs	*am, is, are, have, has, can, will,* etc.
Personal pronouns	*I, me, you, her,* etc.
Possessive pronouns	*his, my, their,* etc.
Relative pronouns	*who(m), whose, that,* etc.

➤ HIGHLIGHTED WORDS

In most sentences, one content word is the most important. This word is highlighted by pronouncing it with the heaviest stress and (usually) highest pitch.

Hère are the kéys.

➤ **STRESS/RHYTHM PATTERNS**

A stress or rhythm pattern refers to the number of syllables and the location of stressed syllables in a word or phrase. The stress/rhythm patterns of words and phrases can be the same:

Stress pattern ◡́◡◡: Óliver all of her

Stress Pattern ◡◡́◡: arríval a ríval

FOCUSED PRACTICE

1 Stress Patterns

Listen to the words and phrases and repeat them. The phrases and sentences in each column have the same rhythm pattern as the underlined word. Concentrate on keeping the rhythm of the phrases in a column the same.

1. volunteer

Who was here?
Take a break.
That's my car.

2. abandon

a garden
I bought it.
They ate them.

3. identification

We met at the station.
I went to the concert.
We needed to take it.

4. demonstration

John's a doctor.
What's the matter?
That's a classic.

5. capability

Who was calling you?
That's illogical.
This is half of it.

6. photographer

a Mexican
I answered it.
He's listening.

2 Apply the Rule

Work with a partner. Circle the content words in the sentences in column A. Then match the sentence with a word in column B that has the same stress/rhythm pattern. Practice saying the sentences.

A	B
____ **1.** She took it.	**a.** vòluntéer
____ **2.** He's visiting.	**b.** idèntificátion
____ **3.** Take a number.	**c.** càpabílity
____ **4.** What's your name?	**d.** abándon
____ **5.** Is that a tomato?	**e.** dèmonstrátion
____ **6.** There's a hospital.	**f.** photógrapher

3 Hearing Rhythm

Listen to the first four lines of Edward Lear's poem, "The Owl and the Pussycat." The stressed syllables are marked for you in the first two lines. Mark the stressed syllables in the second two lines. Then practice saying the poem.

The ówl and the pússycat wént to séa
In a béautiful péa-green bóat
They took some honey and plenty of money
Wrapped up in a five-pound* note.

*British money

4 Rhythm Patterns

A. Listen to the phrases and sentences and repeat them. In the sentences, the underlined words and phrases have the same stress/rhythm pattern as the phrases presented before them.

1. can táke-contáiners: You can táke these contáiners.
2. forgét-for Káte: Don't forgét to buy the book for Káte.
3. Téll her-téller: Téll her that the téller is busy.
4. admíred-at níght: They admíred the city lights at níght.
5. sómeone-cóme when: Did sómeone cóme when you called?
6. to cláss-todáy: I went to cláss todáy.
7. unáble-an áble: I'm unáble to find an áble person for the job.

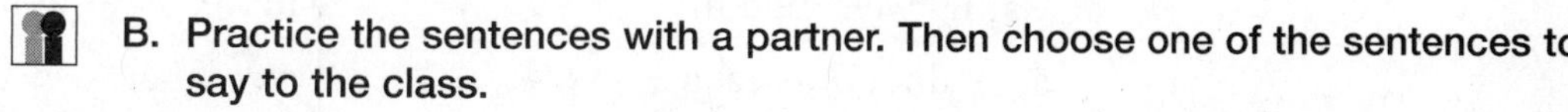

B. Practice the sentences with a partner. Then choose one of the sentences to say to the class.

5 Sounds like . . .

Two phrases that sound the same but have different spellings and meanings are called *homophrases.* Listen to the phrases and repeat them. Then work with a partner to think of a homophrase using a reduced function word. (You can check your answers on page 244.)

1. girls' locket *Girls lock it.*
2. Willy Picket? ______________________
3. Senior class schedule? ______________________

continued

4. the writer left ________________

5. savior stories ________________

6. They conserve water. ________________

7. the dresses in the closet ________________

8. annoys ________________

AND THE OSCAR GOES TO . . .

6 AWARDS, TITLES, AND PRIZES

A. What do you know about these awards? Take this trivia quiz, then check your answers with a partner. (You can check your answers on page 244.)

1. The Clios are awards for
   a. restaurants
   b. theater performances
   c. advertisements
   d. gymnasts

2. The 2000 Summer Olympic Games were held in
   a. Sydney, Australia
   b. Salt Lake City
   c. Seoul
   d. Madrid

3. The Nobel Prize is NOT awarded for achievements in
   a. peace
   b. anthropology
   c. literature
   d. chemistry

4. The Academy Awards began in
   a. 1930
   b. 1927
   c. 1941
   d. 1933

5. Which person has received more Oscar nominations than any other?
   a. Steven Spielberg
   b. Tom Hanks
   c. Walt Disney
   d. Meryl Streep

6. The Emmy Awards are given for
   a. music
   b. movies
   c. television
   d. theater

7. Pulitzer Prizes are awarded for
   a. music
   b. television
   c. writing
   d. medicine

8. Iditarod prizes are given for
   a. a dogsled race in Alaska
   b. a thoroughbred horse race in Florida
   c. breakthroughs in agriculture
   d. software programming

B. Work with a partner. Student A has information about the nomination and voting processes for the People's Choice Movie Awards. Student B has information about how the Academy of Motion Pictures selects Oscar winners. Take notes on what your partner says. Then give a summary of the information back to your partner, using your notes.

Student A's material is on page 249. Student B's material is on page 255.

C. As a class or in small groups, discuss the two movie awards in Part B. Do the names of the awards give a clue about how movies are chosen to win? What are the differences between the procedures for selecting winners? What are the drawbacks of each? The advantages? Which process do you think is better and why?

First listen to:

- Exercises 1 and 4.

Now record them.

Imagine you have won a People's Choice Award or an Oscar for best actor or actress. What would you say? Whom would you thank? Record a brief acceptance speech for your award.

UNIT 34 Highlighting words

INTRODUCTION

In most sentences, one word is the most important. The word may convey new information or correct a previous statement. The most important word is usually highlighted by pronouncing it with the heaviest stress and the highest pitch.

What do you do on the WEEKend?

I get together with FRIENDS.

Beginning a Conversation: When you begin a conversation, you often highlight the last content word.

What did you do on the WEEKend?

Highlighting New Information: New information is often presented in the last content word of a sentence.

(What did you do on the WEEKend?) I went DANcing.

Highlighting Contrasts and Corrections: Highlight information that presents a contrast or corrects a statement. Sentences with contrasts and corrections may have more than one highlighted word.

The mayor's going to RAISE taxes and CUT spending.

The ELEPHANT isn't the largest animal in the world—the WHALE is.

Highlighting Auxiliary Verbs: Highlight auxiliary verbs to show agreement.

A: **This has been a GOOD experience.**

B: **RIGHT. It HAS been a good experience.**

Highlighting Function Words: Function words are normally unstressed, but sometimes we need to emphasize them. Use the full, unreduced form of the function word when you need to highlight it.

(Would you like soup or salad?) I'd like soup AND salad.

FOCUSED PRACTICE

1 DIALOGUES

Listen to the dialogues and repeat them. Circle the highlighted words. Then practice the dialogues with a partner.

1. **A:** I want to pick up my jacket. Here's the ticket.
   B: It's not ready yet. Come back tomorrow.
   A: They said it would be ready today.
   B: I didn't say that. Come back tomorrow.

2. **A:** Why do you like skydiving?
   B: I like the thrill, the rush.
   A: What about fear? Don't you feel afraid?
   B: Sure. But that's part of it. I like the fear.

2 EMPHASIS AND CONTRAST

First read all of the sentences in each set. Then listen to the sentences and circle the highlighted words. Listen again and repeat the sentences.

1. A saying about friendship:
   a. Everyone hears what you say.
   b. Friends listen to what you say.
   c. Best friends listen to what you don't say.

2. Who makes the decisions? The Patels own a small electronics store. Mr. Patel, his wife, and his three children live above the store, and everyone except the baby spends time working in the store. The sentences describe each of the Patels' roles in making decisions about the business.
   a. Mrs. Patel is the real decision maker.
   b. Mr. Patel thinks he makes the decisions.
   c. Jana Patel thinks she ought to make the decisions.
   d. Al Patel doesn't care who makes the decisions.
   e. The baby doesn't even know there is a business.

3 Why Is It?

Work with a partner. Read the questions and circle the words that are being contrasted. Then practice reading the sentences to each other, using heavy stress and high pitch on the contrasted words. (The questions are rhetorical, making fun of the logic of English.)

1. Why does the sun lighten our hair but darken our skin?
2. Why is a boxing ring square?
3. Why is the time of day with the slowest traffic called rush hour?
4. Why isn't there mouse-flavored cat food?
5. Why is the third hand on a clock called the second hand?
6. Why do we drive on parkways and park on driveways?

4 Agreeing

Work with a partner and create short dialogues. Student B shows agreement with Student A's statement by repeating it and highlighting the auxiliary verb.

EXAMPLE

A: You drive too slowly.

B: { Yes / Right. / I agree. } I DO drive too slowly.

1. Susana should win the prize.
2. The essay was well written.
3. Rafael looks a lot like his brother.
4. The final exam will cover a lot of material.
5. They've been gone a long time.
6. That new student's really cute.

5 LISTENING: *"Thrill Seekers"*

A. Before you listen, make sure you understand this vocabulary:

(to) pound	palms	butterflies in your stomach	
crave	adrenaline rush	roller coaster	hair-raising

B. Listen to "Thrill Seekers" and fill in the blanks with the highlighted words you hear.

Everyone knows what it's like to feel ____________ scared. Your ____________ pounds, you ____________ faster, your ____________ sweat, you get ____________ in your stomach.

Psychologist Frank Farley has studied people who like to live life "on the edge." He coined the term "type T" to describe their personalities: They are ____________ seekers. They crave the ____________ and ____________ of activities that ____________ of us consider ____________ terrifying or dangerous. They enjoy the ____________ sensations that ____________ fear—the adrenaline rush and the racing heart. According to Farley, type T's have high levels of ____________ and self-____________. They believe their fate is in *their* hands and that life is not worth living if they are not being ____________.

C. Work with a partner. Read the sentences, and then decide which words should be highlighted. Practice reading the sentences to each other.

1. Many people enjoy the thrill of safe fear, but others need more.
2. Type T personalities crave both the mental intensity and physical sensations of fear.
3. Roller coasters are hair-raising rides; merry-go-rounds are tame.
4. Hiking is a relatively safe sport; rock climbing is more dangerous.
5. Jumping off a diving board is fun; bungee-jumping off a bridge is crazy.
6. If you're skydiving, your fate isn't in your hands; it's in your parachute.

6 INTERVIEWS

Look at the list of activities in the chart. Check the ones you've done or would like to try. Then interview two other classmates to see which of these activities they enjoy or would like to try. Share your results with the class. Are there any type T's among you?

	You	Student 1 ______	Student 2 ______
Watching horror movies			
Reading scary books/stories			
Bungee-jumping			
Skydiving			
Sky surfing			
Downhill skiing			
Snowboarding			
Rock climbing			
Mountain biking			
Dirt bike racing			
Riding roller coasters/ scary rides			
Surfing			
Windsurfing			
Other ______			

First listen to:

- Exercise 2.

Now record it.

Look at the list of activities in Exercise 6. Choose four and give your opinion of them. Have you ever tried them? Would you ever? Why or why not?

UNIT 35

Thought groups
Thought groups and intonation
Joining thought groups

INTRODUCTION

➤ THOUGHT GROUPS

Group the words of a sentence into shorter phrases, or *thought groups.* Thought groups help the listener identify the parts of a sentence; they help the speaker by breaking the sentence into shorter parts.

I don't understand the new rules.

➤ LENGTH OF THOUGHT GROUPS

There are no fixed rules for deciding what the thought groups of a sentence are. When you are learning a language, it is better to use shorter thought groups because they give you more time to plan what you want to say. Look at the two ways the words in this sentence can be grouped together.

If you want to get ahead, dress for success.

If you want to get ahead, dress for success.

➤ THOUGHT GROUPS AND INTONATION

There is usually a small rise or fall in pitch at the end of a thought group. The change in pitch isn't as great as it is at the end of a sentence.

If you want to get ahead, dress for success.

If you wear a suit, you'll look stuffy.

➤ JOINING THOUGHT GROUPS TOGETHER

Hold the last word of a thought group briefly before you begin the next.

I didn't get the job because of my tattoo. (hold briefly)

That cashier wears a nose ring. (hold briefly)

➤ THOUGHT GROUPS AND GRAMMATICAL PHRASES

Thought groups often correspond to grammatical phrases.

Prepositional phrases	in a mínute	at the aírport
Verb + Pronoun	búy them	bríng it
Determiner + Noun	my úncle	the párk
Short clauses	When you léave,	cáll me.

FOCUSED PRACTICE

1 LIMERICKS

A limerick is a humorous five-line poem with a specific rhythm.

Listen to the limerick and repeat it. Underline the thought groups, and then practice saying the limerick with a partner.

A mouse in her room woke Miss Dowd.
She was frightened and screamed very loud.
Then a happy thought hit her
To scare off the critter—
She sat up in bed and meowed.

2 ADVICE COLUMN

Listen to the recording and fill in the blanks. Then practice reading the letters with a partner. Group words together when you speak.

Dear MJ,

I'm preparing for an ____________ job interview with a business that has a ____________, youthful image. Should I wear something traditional, like a ____________? Or should I ____________ ____________ something more trendy? I don't want to ____________ "stuffy," but I don't want them to think that I think I ____________ have the job.

Standing in Front of My Closet

Dear Standing,

Go with ____________. If you get the job, you can ____________ whatever style the business has. But traditional business clothes ____________ competence and dedication. Plus, if you ____________ the job, the ____________ may be the last time you can wear your suit.

MJ

3 Differences in Meaning

The way you group words in a sentence can affect the meaning.

A. Listen to the pairs of sentences and repeat them. Group words to show the different meanings in the sentence pairs. Then listen again and circle the letter of the sentence you hear.

1. a. "Max," replied Susan, "why don't you wear a suit?"
   b. Max replied, "Susan, why don't you wear a suit?"

2. a. There are five, year-old bottles of wine in the basement.
   b. There are five-year-old bottles of wine in the basement.

3. a. Stanley asked Stella, "How long is your sister going to stay?"
   b. "Stanley," asked Stella, "how long is your sister going to stay?"

4. a. Why are you going to leave Bob?
   b. Why are you going to leave, Bob?

5. a. The teacher said we'd have two, hour-long tests.
   b. The teacher said we'd have two-hour-long tests.

6. a. My sister, who lives in Boston, is coming tomorrow.
   b. My sister who lives in Boston is coming tomorrow.

B. Work with a partner and take turns. Choose a sentence from Part A and say it to your partner. Group words clearly so your partner can tell you which sentence you said.

DRESS FOR SUCCESS

4 Dressing Down or Dressing Up?

Read the paragraph below and underline thought groups. Then compare your thought groups with a partner's (they may not be the same). Practice reading the paragraph to each other, grouping words as you marked them.

Some businesses are returning to a more conservative, formal style of dressing in the workplace. David Goodfellow, CEO of Maritage, Inc., says the return to more formal dress in the office has improved the quality of business meetings and discussions. In a survey of 1,000 companies, over 40 percent reported that more relaxed dress codes were accompanied by an increase in employee lateness and absenteeism.

(taken from "Some employers boot business casual," by Jennie L. Phillps, April 20, 2001, bankrate.com)

5 Listening: *"Business Dress Codes"*

A. Before you listen, make sure you understand this vocabulary:

tattoos	body piercing	(to) sport a nose ring
come under fire	ban	Sikh
dreadlocks	Rastafarian	infringe upon someone's rights

B. Listen to the recording. Then connect the phrases in the three columns so that they make separate, complete sentences that summarize the information in the recording. Read your sentences with a partner.

A	B	C
A Sikh job applicant	at a Safeway store	has tattoos all over his arms.
A typical student	at Ideal Market	had to cover his tattoo.
A health care worker	at any college in the country	has tattoos and body piercings.
A popular cashier	at a California facility	wasn't hired because he wouldn't shave his beard.
A Rastafarian worker	at Lexmart International	doesn't have to cut his dreadlocks.
A computer worker	at Domino's Pizza	wears a nose ring.

6 DRESS CODES

Appropriate appearance in the workplace depends on a variety of factors and is different in different countries. Think about dress codes in your country. Which items in the chart would be appropriate for bank employees, athletes, students, and food service workers in your country? Talk about your answers as a class or in small groups.

	Bank employees	Athletes	Students	Food service workers
Body art				
Tattoos				
Pierced ears (multiple holes/ear)				
Nose rings				
Eyebrow rings				
Clothing				
Torn jeans				
Jeans				
Sneakers				
Halter tops				
Stretch pants/leggings				
Suits and ties (men)				
Suits, dresses/skirts (women)				
Uniforms				

First listen to:

- Exercise 1.

Now record it.

If you were an employer, what kind of dress code would you require of your employees? Make a one-minute recording explaining your answer. Include information about the type of business you are describing.

UNIT 36 Rhythm patterns: personal pronouns

INTRODUCTION

➤ SUBJECT PRONOUNS

Subject pronouns are usually unstressed.

He ásked when I wánted to gó.

Reductions of Subject Pronouns. Before contractions of *will* (*'ll*) and *are* (*'re*), the vowels in pronouns may be reduced.

I'll dó it. (sounds like "all")

She'll dó it. (rhymes with "still")

We're hére. ([wɪr], [wər])

They're góne. (sounds like "there")

➤ OBJECT PRONOUNS

Object pronouns are pronounced like endings on the preceding verb.

Open it. Read them.

Reductions of Object Pronouns. Inside a sentence, *them* is pronounced with the reduced vowel [ə].

I bought them. [ðəm]

➤ PRONOUNS BEGINNING WITH *h*

Pronouns beginning with [h] lose [h] inside a sentence.

call him ("callim")

What did he do? (What "diddy" do?)

This is her office. (This "izzer" office.)

➤ FAST SPEECH REDUCTIONS

The reductions described above are common to all styles of English. Native speakers also make other reductions to pronouns in informal speech. You should be aware of these reductions.

Listen to the reductions.

1. *You* in common expressions.

***you* after** [t, d]	***you* after other sounds**
Where "didjə" go? (Where did you go?)	"Seeyə" later. (See you later.)
I won't "letchə" go. (I won't let you go.)	I'll "callyə" tonight. (I'll call you tonight.)

2. *Them* may be reduced to [əm].

Did you "findəm" at the store? (Did you find them at the store?)

FOCUSED PRACTICE

1 REDUCED *h* WORDS

Listen to the dialogues and fill in the blanks. Cross out unpronounced [h] in *he, him, his, her, have, has,* and *had.* Then practice the dialogues with a partner.

1. **A:** Why ____________ ____________ sold ____________ house?
   B: She's ____________ back home to stay with ____________ mother.
2. **A:** Would ____________ tell Professor Sommers ____________ bring ____________ my paper tomorrow?
   B: Why ____________? Why don't ____________ tell ____________ ____________?
3. **A:** The lawyer said to meet ____________ at ____________ office tomorrow with the papers.
   B: What does ____________ want ____________ to bring?
4. **A:** Please tell Mr. Blake ____________ a call for ____________.
   B: I don't know ____________ ____________ in or not.

2 Instant Messages

Instant messaging through the Internet makes use of abbreviations and often omits function words and punctuation.

Work with a partner. Read the instant messages. Write the messages in the blanks using normal spelling. Add words when necessary. (You can check your answers on page 244.)

Nightgloom: Palerider u there? ____________________

Palerider: Wassup? ____________________

Nightgloom: talked 2 sue 2day. She likes u. me 2.

____

Palerider: i like u2. Sue said she likes me?

____

Nightgloom: y ____________________

Palerider: working. gtg* ____________________

Nightgloom: ok C U tmw ____________________

Palerider: C U 2. bye. ____________________

Nightgloom: bye ____________________

**gtg:* got to go

3 Hearing Reduced Pronouns

Listen to the sentences and repeat them. Then practice the sentences with a partner. The pairs of underlined words have the same or nearly the same pronunciation.

1. Oliver Hart recorded "All of Her Heart."
2. Put the books I bought him on the bottom shelf.
3. Would he like to meet Woody Harrelson?
4. The sailor agreed to sail her boat in the race.
5. Lee's seen your senior prom* pictures.
6. The old concrete wall is too porous* so the builder is going to pour us a new wall.

**prom:* a dance for seniors in high school; *porous:* allowing substances to pass through

4 QUOTATIONS

On Halloween of 1938, a group of actors performed a radio play based on H. G. Wells's novel, *The War of the Worlds,* which described an invasion of the earth by aliens from Mars. The radio play was written like a news broadcast, so many listeners believed it was real and panicked.

Seven million Americans heard the radio broadcast of *War of the Worlds.* One million believed that the United States was actually being invaded by Martians. Sociologist Hadley Cantril studied this case of mass panic and interviewed many people. These sentences are quotations from some of the Americans whom Hadley interviewed.

Read the quotations and fill in the blanks with pronouns. Compare your answers with a partner. Then choose a sentence and say it to the class.

1. My husband tried to calm ____*me*____ and said, "If this were so, ____*it*____ would be on all the stations."
2. When I heard that poison gas was in the streets of Newark, I called my brother and his wife and told ____________ to come right over.
3. My son came home during the excitement and I sent ____________ out to see what ____________ was all about.
4. I couldn't stand ____________ so I turned ____________ off.
5. I was writing a history paper. The girl from upstairs came and made ____________ go up to her place.
6. When I got home, my husband wasn't there so I rushed to the neighbors to tell ____________ the world was coming to an end.
7. I heard the announcer say that ____________ saw a Martian standing in the middle of Times Square. . . . That's all I had to hear—I knew ____________ had to be a play.
8. It was so real. . . . But I turned to WOR [another radio station] to see if they had the same thing on. They didn't, so I knew ____________ must be a fake.

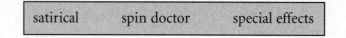

5 LISTENING: *"Wag the Dog"*

A. Before you listen, make sure you understand this vocabulary:

satirical	spin doctor	special effects

B. Listen to the recording. Then, as a class or in small groups, answer these questions:

1. Who did the scandal involve?
2. When was the scandal uncovered?
3. Why was a spin doctor called into the White House?
4. Do you think the public today could be fooled into believing in a fictional crisis? Why or why not?

First listen to:

- Exercise 1.

Now record it.

Think about these questions and record your answers:

Why did so many people believe *War of the Worlds* was a real news broadcast?

Do you think the people of 1938 were more *gullible,* or easily fooled, than people of today?

UNIT 37 Rhythm patterns: articles

INTRODUCTION

Articles (*a, an,* or *the*) are unstressed. They are pronounced in a thought group with the following noun.

a mán   an ónion   the wéather

➤ *THE*

The **is often pronounced [ðiy] before a vowel. The [y] of [ðiy] joins to the following noun. Be sure to pronounce the *th* of *the* correctly.** **the_áir** [ðiy ɛr]   **the_ócean** [ðiy owʃən]
The **is pronounced [ðə] before a consonant.** **the bóok** [ðə] **book**   **the pláce** [ðə] **place**

➤ *A, AN*

Reduce the vowel of *a/an* to [ə]. *An* joins closely to the following word. **a peninsula** [ə]   **an_island** [ən]
Be careful with words that begin with the letter *u*. In words like *union* and *useful,* the first sound is the consonant [y] and the article is *a*. **a union member**   **a useful tool**

FOCUSED PRACTICE

1 Apply the Rule

How is *the* pronounced in these sentences? Write "ə" or "iy" in the blank to show the pronunciation of *the.* Then practice saying the sentences with a partner. Use clear thought groups and pronounce *the* correctly.

1. I met the author. __iy__
2. Canada is the biggest country in North America. ______
3. What's the answer? ______
4. Did you use the method in the book? ______
5. When did the United States become a country? ______
6. I didn't understand the unit on articles. ______

2 Apply the Rule

Write *a* or *an* in the blank. Then practice saying the phrases with a partner. Join words together and reduce the vowel of *a/an* to [ə].

1. __an__ announcement
2. ___ utopia
3. ___ continent
4. ___ peninsula
5. ___ island
6. ___ harbor
7. ___ honest man
8. ___ universal truth
9. ___ mountain range
10. ___ university town

3 Sounds Like . . .

Two phrases that sound the same (or nearly the same) but have different spellings and meanings are called *homophrases.* Listen to these homophrases and repeat them. Then work with a partner to think of a homophrase that includes an article. (You can check your answers on page 244.)

1. announce __an ounce__
2. arrested suspect ______
3. arrival city ______
4. attention ______
5. apparent reasons ______
6. unattractive style ______

4 THE PLACE NAME GAME

Divide the class into two groups, Team 1 and Team 2. Team 1 asks questions of Team 2, and vice versa. The questions are all about places. Each group decides whether to use *the* with the place name in the question and answer. The team that is answering questions receives a point for each correct answer correctly pronounced. (Guidelines for using *the* with place names are given in the box.)

Using *the* with place names	
Use *the* with	**Do not use *the* with**
• country names that include words like *United, State, Republic, Union*	• most country names
• names of buildings	• most city names
• names of mountain ranges	• state names
• names of groups of islands	• names of single mountains
• names of groups of lakes	• names of single islands
• names of bridges	• names of single lakes
	• names of continents

Team 1's questions are on page 249; Team 2's questions are on page 256.

EXAMPLE 1 White House (city)

A: *Where's the White House? Name the city.*

B: *In Washington, D.C.*

EXAMPLE 2 Texas (country)

A: *Where's Texas? Name the country.*

B: *In the United States.*

5 LISTENING: *"Aging Populations"*

A. First read the passage. Fill in the blanks with *a, an, the,* or nothing. Then listen to the recording. Check your answers and correct them if necessary.

__________ world's population is graying. Demographers, sociologists, and economists have known this for __________ long time. What is new today, according to Joseph Chamie, __________ director of __________ UN's Population Division, is __________ pace at which __________ world is aging.

By 2050, __________ number of __________ people living to __________ age of 100 will be fifteen times higher than it is today. In 2050, one person in five will be 60 or older; by 2150, __________ number will increase to one in every three people. In __________ developed countries, __________ increase will happen even faster. One of __________ reasons that __________ older people account for __________ larger proportion of __________ population is __________ decline in __________ birth rates in many countries. __________ aging population presents both __________ challenges and opportunities to __________ society.

B. Listen to some of the highlights from the UN report and take notes. Then use your notes to answer these questions. Use complete sentences in your answers.

1. What country has the oldest median (most common) age? What is the age?

____

____

____

2. What are some other "old" countries mentioned on the tape?

____

____

____

3. What will happen to the ratio of women to men as populations age?

____

____

____

4. What is expected to happen in Singapore and Costa Rica?

____

____

____

C. In small groups, discuss these questions:

What are some of the challenges that countries with large numbers of older people face?

What opportunities do older people create for a society/economy?

Why do you think birth rates are falling in most countries?

In your country, is the population as a whole growing? Is the government concerned about population growth/decline in your country?

First listen to:

- Exercise 5.

Now record it.

Make a one-minute recording describing the city or town where you live. Include any famous or important buildings, natural landmarks such as mountains, lakes, and rivers, and any other important or interesting information. Use *the* with place names when needed, and pronounce it correctly in each case.

UNIT 38 Rhythm patterns: prepositional phrases *"Hafta, gonna, wanna"*

INTRODUCTION

"Short" prepositions (*to, at, in, on, for, of, with, from*) are unstressed and pronounced with the following noun.

at hóme   to cláss   on tíme

In some cases, the preposition has become part of the next word: *forever, tomorrow.*

The prepositions *at* and *for* are usually reduced to [ət] and [fər].

I study at night.
[ət]

I had eggs for breakfast.
[fər]

***Of* can be pronounced [ə] before a consonant. It is usually pronounced [əv] before a vowel.**

a cup of coffee
"a cuppə coffee"

the end of August
"əv August"

***To* has two pronunciations, depending on the following sound.**

1. **Before consonants, pronounce *to* as [tə].**

   to schóol
   "tə school"

   to wórk
   "tə work"

2. **Before vowels, *to* is usually pronounced [tuw].**

   to a restaurant
   "[tuw] a restaurant"

➤ "STRANDED" PREPOSITIONS

Stranded prepositions are prepositions that are "left" at the end of a sentence or phrase:

Who(m) did you talk to?

In this question, *to* is a "stranded" preposition.

Stranded prepositions are not stressed but their vowels are not reduced.

What are you looking at?
[æt]

➤ STRESSED PREPOSITIONS

In two-word verbs, prepositions are used as adverbs and are stressed. (See Unit 39 for more on two-word verbs.)

Come ÓN. Pick it ÚP. Watch ÓUT.

➤ *HAFTA, GONNA, WANNA*

Have to/has to are pronounced as one word: [hæftə, hæstə].

I have to pay my bills. **She has to work tonight.**
"haftə" **"hastə"**

Gonna is a fast speech reduction of the future auxiliary _going to._ This pronunciation is common in informal English.

This year I'm gonna lose weight.

- ***Gonna* includes *to.* If you use *gonna,* do NOT add another *to:***

This year I'm gonna ~~to~~ study more.

- **Do NOT use *gonna* when *going* is the main verb:**

We're going to Cleveland. (not "gonna")

Wanna is a fast speech reduction of _want to_ or _want a._ This pronunciation is common in informal English.

Do you *wanna* go shopping? **Do you *wanna* sandwich?**
(want to) **(want a)**

FOCUSED PRACTICE

1 PREPOSITIONS

Read the sentences and fill in the blanks with logical prepositions. Then listen to the sentences to check your answers. Listen again and repeat the sentences. Reduce prepositions and group words together. Practice the sentences with a partner.

1. **a.** I spent $143 _______ a date last night.
   b. I paid $85 _______ dinner _______ a restaurant and $8 _______ a valet _______ park my car.
   c. Afterwards, _______ a night club, I spent another $44 _______ two rounds _______ drinks and another $6 _______ valet parking.
   d. I put everything _______ my credit card, except _______ the valet parking. I paid _______ that _______ cash.

2. **a.** I was going _______ go _______ the doctor's _______ two o'clock today.
   b. My appointment was cancelled because the doctor had _______ be _______ the hospital _______ a patient.
   c. So I decided _______ go _______ the mall _______ celebrate the cancellation.
   d. I saw some shoes I liked _______ a shoe store but they weren't _______ sale.

2 HEARING REDUCTIONS

Listen to the sentences and repeat them. The underlined words have similar or identical pronunciations. Then practice the sentences with a partner.

1. I brought tamales* to Molly's.
2. You have to take this letter to the deputy consul at the consulate.
3. I keep forgetting to thank you for getting the party supplies.
4. You were considerate to deliver the plans we'll consider at work.
5. The officer who performed the act of courage is on active duty in Atlanta.
6. She has the ability to explain indelicate matters in delicate language.

**tamales:* a Mexican dish

3 SOUNDS LIKE . . .

Two phrases that sound the same but have different spellings and meanings are called *homophrases.* Listen to these homophrases and repeat them. Then work with a partner to think of a homophrase that includes a reduced preposition. (You can check your answers on page 244.)

1. He saved a fortunate school. *He saved a fortune at school.*
2. They explained these incredible terms. ____________
3. That's a divisive technology. ____________
4. I don't believe indirect advice. ____________
5. The legislation was passed by an active Congress. ____________

____

4 FULL OR REDUCED?

Listen to the recording and write the pronunciation you hear. Before you listen, make sure you understand this vocabulary:

hafta	hasta	gonna	going to	wanna	want(s) the

1. If you *wanna* come with us, you'll ____________ hurry because we're ____________ leave in five minutes.
2. My roommates ____________ make spaghetti so I'm ____________ the store.
3. Do you ____________ report now or do you ____________ wait until later?
4. Maria ____________ notes from yesterday's class because she ____________ study.
5. Are you ____________ the library tonight or do you ____________ go out?
6. My credit card is maxed out.* I'm ____________ ____________ pay it off.

**maxed out:* charged to the maximum limit (slang)

MEN, WOMEN, AND MONEY

5 LISTENING: *"Men Buy and Women Shop"*

Here are the results of a study on how men and women regard money.

A. Listen to the recording and complete the chart. If more women than men said a statement, check the "Women" column; if more men than women said it, check the "Men" column. If it's equally true for men and women, check both columns.

	Women	Men	You
I worry about money.			
Money worries interfere with my work.			
Money worries interfere with my relationships.			
I'm worried about my level of savings.			
I buy things I don't need.			
I can't resist a sale.			
I use shopping to celebrate or feel better.			
I sometimes hide my spending.			

B. Work in a small group. Read the statements in the chart again and check those that are true for you. Do the results of the study reflect your attitude toward money and shopping?

First listen to:

- Exercises 1 and 2.

Now record them.

Compare your answers in the chart in Exercise 5 with the results from the study. Are your answers typical for your sex? Why do you think the researchers found differences for men and women?

UNIT 39 Rhythm patterns: two-word verbs

INTRODUCTION

➤ TWO-WORD VERBS

Two-word verbs are verbs followed by prepositions. The preposition functions as an adverb and is not reduced. Two-word verbs often have a special meaning:

Two-word verb	**Verb + Preposition**
Come ón! Let's go.	They usually come on the bus.
(*come on* means "hurry up" here)	

➤ STRESS IN TWO-WORD VERBS

1. The verb and preposition are separated.

- **Both the verb and preposition can be stressed.**

  Lóok the wórd úp. **Thrów thése óut tomórrow.**

- **The preposition may be stressed more heavily than the verb when it ends a sentence or clause or when a pronoun separates the verb and preposition.**

  Lòok it úp. **Pùt it óff.** **Dò them óver.**

2. The verb and preposition are not separated.

- **Either the verb or the preposition has heavy stress, but not both. The choice often depends on the overall rhythm of the sentence.**

  I don't want to páy off my loan.

  I've just paid óff my loan.

➤ NOUNS FORMED FROM TWO-WORD VERBS

Use compound noun stress: Stress the first word heavily and pronounce it with high pitch; use secondary stress and lower pitch on the second word.

Tákeòff's been delayed an hour. He had a nervous bréakdòwn.

FOCUSED PRACTICE

1 Sentences with Two-Word Verbs

Listen to the sentences and repeat them. Group words together and join consonants to vowels.

1. Our tákeoff was smooth even though we took óff in a storm.
2. Hand it ín when you've filled it óut.
3. I'm not going to cléan up the kitchen because I didn't mess it úp.
4. Please call him úp before you go óut.
5. Did you fínd out why they cálled off the interview?
6. I didn't like the coat when I tried it ón.

2 Dialogues

Listen to the dialogues and repeat them. Two-word verbs are underlined. Then practice the dialogues with a partner. Group words together and speak smoothly.

1. **A:** I've already picked the application up. Should I fill it out now or drop it off later?

   B: Fill it out now if you have time. Otherwise bring it back by tomorrow.

2. **A:** It looks like rain now, but it's supposed to clear up later. Let's leave now.

   B: You go on without me. I'll catch up with you later.

3. **A:** It's time to clean up the apartment. I'll take out the garbage and straighten up the living room.

   B: I'll bundle the newspapers up and clean out the refrigerator.

4. **A:** Can you help me with this math problem? I've done it over twice and I still can't figure it out.

   B: You've written it down wrong. This number should be 4, not 3. Try it again. It'll come out right.

3 Complete the Dialogues

Work with a partner and complete the dialogues with two-word verbs from the box, adding pronouns when necessary. You may need to use a verb more than once or use it as a noun. Then practice the dialogues.

make up	throw out	put off	call up	bring back	try out

1. **A:** Do you have Anton's number? I need to tell him the schedule has changed.
   B: I've already ________________.
2. **A:** I don't want to finish this now. Maybe I'll wait till tomorrow.
   B: You shouldn't ________________. You won't have time tomorrow.
3. **A:** Thanks for letting me borrow your book. When will you need it?
   B: Could you ________________ tomorrow?
4. **A:** Do you want any of these old papers?
   B: No. Go ahead and ________________.
5. **A:** I've decided to ________________ for the lead role in the play.
   B: When are the ________________s?
6. **A:** When are you going to ________________ the test you missed?
   B: I've already ________________.

4 Hearing Stress with Prepositions

Listen to the sentences and mark stressed prepositions with a stress mark. Compare your work with a partner. Then listen again and repeat the sentences.

1. Do it if you want to. The decision is up to you.
2. He didn't ask us in. He made us wait for him on the porch.
3. The military took over the government buildings. After the takeover, we were afraid to leave our homes.
4. Come on! Let's take the day off.
5. I look up to people who look information up when they can't figure something out.

JAMES BOND AND GI JOE

5 LISTENING: *"007's Toys"*

A. Read the passage and fill in the blanks with logical prepositions. Then listen to the recording to check your work.

Dennis Wend works ______ the army ______ its National Automotive Center ______ Detroit, Michigan. It's Wend's job ______ come ______ ______ cutting-edge technology ______ army vehicles. One day Wend was watching a James Bond thriller and he asked himself, "How come we have this kind ______ technology ______ the movies and we haven't looked ______ it ______ our soldiers?"

So Wend's team set ______ ______ build a vehicle 007 would be proud ______. They created the SmarTruck, a truck that looks like an SUV that's been raised ______ growth hormones. The purpose ______ the truck is ______ provide protection. So what can the SmarTruck do?

The truck comes ______ a special fingerprint and ring detector, which only allows authorized people ______ turn it ______. If the SmarTruck runs ______ trouble, it can defend itself. A few ______ its many defenses include electrified door handles and pepper spray that shoots ______ the back ______ the car. There's also a 360-degree camera that watches ______ ______ trouble, a laser gun, and a nozzle that sprays ______ a cloud ______ fog.

As for looks, the SmarTruck is no match ______ 007's Lotus Turbo Esprit. But it has a different kind ______ appeal ______ its jet-black paint and muscular build: It would definitely create an impression coming ______ the highway ______ rush hour.

B. Practice reading the passage with a partner.

6 THE GADGET GAME

Two-word verbs are often used in descriptions of machines and gadgets.

A. Think of a machine or gadget (for example, CD player, computer, hair dryer, can opener) and think of two-word verbs that describe it or how it works. Here are some possible verbs to help you:

turn up	turn down	turn on	turn off
clean up	throw away (out)	pick up	put down
put in	take off	take out	put on

B. Work with a partner. Describe the machine or gadget you've chosen to your partner without using its name and without using your hands. Your partner will guess what the gadget is.

EXAMPLE

A: I'm thinking of something that's used for writing. When an old one is **used up,** you **throw it away.**

B: Is it a pen?

A: Yes, it is!

First listen to:

- Exercise 1.

Now record it.

Think of three machines or gadgets. Record a description of them and how they work. Use as many two-word verbs as you can.

UNIT 40 Rhythm patterns: *as, than, if*

INTRODUCTION

➤ **UNSTRESSED CONJUNCTIONS: *as, than, if***

***As* is unstressed and reduced to [əz]. Join *as* to the surrounding words.** **I've dóne as múch as I cán.** [əz] [əz]
***Than* is unstressed and reduced to [ðən].** **Is Énglish hárder than Chinése?** [ðən]
***If* is unstressed and pronounced with the words following or preceding it.** **Pléase cóme if you háve tíme.**

FOCUSED PRACTICE

1 CONJUNCTIONS

Listen to the sentences and repeat them. Speak smoothly.

1. Be careful if you go out. The sidewalk is as slippery as greased glass.
2. The fleece on Mary's prize lamb was as white as snow.
3. After her mother's death, she felt a sadness as deep as the ocean.
4. The college had more applications last year than ever before.
5. She wondered if he'd ever call again.
6. Do women spend more time on the phone than men?
7. Maybe. But they don't spend as much time watching TV.
8. What lives if you feed it and dies if you water it? Fire.
9. Goran frowned and said, "Taking drugs is as dangerous as playing with fire."

2 Dialogues

Work with a partner to complete these dialogues. Then practice the dialogues with your partner.

1. **A:** Karen's been sick so long she's as weak as _a kitten_.
   B: The doctor doesn't know if ______________________.
2. **A:** Don't tell Mom, but her cookies taste worse than ______________________.
   B: Try her cake! It's as dry as ______________________.
3. **A:** The questions on that test were trickier than ______________________.
   B: And it lasted longer than ______________________.
4. **A:** A storm's coming. The sky is getting as black as ______________________.
   B: Let's go in. Your hands are colder than ______________________.

3 Similes

Writers use similes to show that two different things are similar. Similes with *as* + adjective + *as* also occur in expressions to show that something possesses a high degree of the adjective: *I'm as hungry as a bear* means "I'm very hungry."

Work in a small group. Match the adjectives in column A with the nouns in column B to come up with common English similes using *as . . . as.* Take turns reading the similes. Reduce *as* and join it to the surrounding words.

	A	B	Simile
_c_	**1.** hungry	**a.** grass	_He's as hungry as a bear._
___	**2.** good	**b.** peacock*	______________
___	**3.** shy/quiet	**c.** bear	______________
___	**4.** fat	**d.** mule	______________
___	**5.** sly/clever	**e.** penny	______________
___	**6.** bright	**f.** gold	______________
___	**7.** stubborn	**g.** mouse	______________
___	**8.** proud	**h.** pig	______________
___	**9.** green	**i.** fox	______________

**peacock:* a large bird in brilliant turquoise colors that spreads its tail feathers like a fan

4 Riddles

Riddles are word puzzles that ask a question.

Work with a partner and take turns. Each of you has three riddles. Read a riddle to your partner. Your partner will guess the answer. You can give hints if necessary.

EXAMPLE

A: What belongs to you, but others use it more than you do?

B: *Your name.*

Student A's riddles are on page 250. Student B's riddles are on page 256.

BRILLIANT!

5 Listening: *"Geniuses"*

A genius is defined as someone with an IQ score (the score on a special intelligence test) of over 140. Because geniuses are rare, many people believe that they are "stranger" than normal people. Psychologist Lewis Terman studied child geniuses to find out whether popular beliefs about geniuses were true.

A. Listen to the recording. Take notes on the nine misconceptions about geniuses that Lewis Terman found in his study.

____

____

____

____

____

B. Use your notes to write sentences about three of the misconceptions mentioned in the recording. Use *as, than,* or *if* in your sentences. Read a sentence to the class and explain the misconception.

1. ______________________________

2. ______________________________

3. ______________________________

6 STANDARDIZED TESTS

Standardized tests are tests that all students must take to get into (or out of) schools. The tests usually have several sections, each of which must be completed in a certain amount of time.

A. The chart presents information on some standardized tests students take to enter U.S. colleges and graduate or professional schools. Write four sentences about the tests in the chart. Use *as*, *if*, or *than* in your sentences.

Test	Who takes it?	Test content	Cost (2002)	Time
SAT (say, "S-A-T")	High school students applying to college	General verbal and quantitative skills	Varies depending on number of colleges scores are sent to	3 hours
TOEFL (say, "toe-full")	Nonnative speakers of English	Listening, structure, vocabulary, writing	$110	3.5–4 hours
GRE (say, "G-R-E")	College students applying to graduate schools	Verbal and quantitative reasoning; writing	$115	2 hours 15 minutes
GMAT (say, "G-mat")	College students applying to MBA programs	General verbal and quantitative skills; analytic writing	$200	4 hours
LSAT (say, "L-sat")	College students applying to law schools	Reading and verbal reasoning; writing	$103	Half day
MCAT (say, "M-cat")	College students applying to medical schools	Verbal reasoning, physical and biological science; writing	$185	Full day

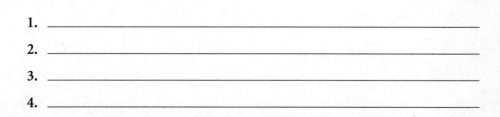

1. ______________________________
2. ______________________________
3. ______________________________
4. ______________________________

 **B. Read your sentences to a partner. Then discuss standardized tests. Have you or your partner ever taken one of these tests? What was your experience?**

First listen to:

- Exercise 1.

Now record it.

Record answers to these questions: Have you ever taken a standardized test? If so, what was your experience? Do you prefer timed, short-answer tests or longer, essay-style tests? Does taking a test make you nervous?

UNIT 41 Rhythm patterns: *that* Consonant clusters with "TH" Intonation and clauses

INTRODUCTION

➤ STRESSED AND UNSTRESSED *THAT*

That is stressed and pronounced [ðæt] when it is a demonstrative pronoun or adjective.

Thát's ríght.   Thát mán.   Thát one.   I dón't líke thát.

That is unstressed and reduced to [ðət] when it is a conjunction.

Thís méans that I'm ríght.
[ðət]

The Spánish explórers belíeved that Sóuth América was fúll of góld.
[ðət]

Grouping *that*. When *that* is a conjunction, it is usually grouped with words in the following clause.

Is it true that Americans eat only fast food?

➤ CONSONANT CLUSTERS WITH TH

When *that* is followed by *the*, a difficult cluster occurs at the boundary between the two words: *that **the*** [tð]. Pronounce both consonants, without separating them.

Péople wórry that the envíronment is in dánger.

➤ INTONATION AND CLAUSES

There is usually a change in intonation to mark a boundary between two clauses. Intonation often rises a little at the end of one phrase/clause.

She said that it was important.

Sometimes intonation may fall a little at the end of the first clause.

He told me a story that I don't believe.

FOCUSED PRACTICE

1 Reduced *that*

Listen to the sentences and repeat them. Group words together. Then practice reading the sentences with a partner.

1. Which man? The man that left?
2. She insisted that they practice.
3. I told him that I couldn't come.
4. He said that he could come.
5. Is it true that tea with lemon gets rid of a cold?
6. I don't think that it's true.

2 Stressed and Unstressed *that*

Listen to the sentences. Put a stress mark over *that* if it is used as a demonstrative adjective or pronoun. Then listen again and repeat the sentences. Choose a sentence and say it to the class.

1. Did you buy that coat that I showed you?
2. He said that that one wasn't working.
3. That car that that woman drives used to be mine.
4. That's the one that I want.
5. Did you like that movie that you saw?
6. Don't forget that that program is on TV tonight.

3 TH Sounds

Listen to the sentences and repeat them. Underline words that have TH sounds. Then practice the sentences with a partner.

1. Spanish explorers in the 1500s believed that the "city of gold," El Dorado, lay somewhere in the mountains of South America.
2. Some people say that the Pacific Northwest is the home of Bigfoot, a huge hairy creature that's half man, half beast.
3. In the late 1600s in Salem, Massachusetts, several people were hanged because they refused to say that they were witches.
4. A sailor's superstition says that the albatross, a large bird, is unlucky.

4 Definitions

Work with a partner. Match the words in column A with the definitions in column B. Then take turns asking questions and giving definitions. Speak smoothly, grouping words together.

EXAMPLE

A: What's *a clock?*

B: *A clock is something that tells time.*

A	B
b 1. a clock (something)	a. has circular winds
___ 2. a battery (something)	b. tells time
___ 3. a bat (an animal)	c. dispenses cash
___ 4. a glider (a plane)	d. combines breakfast and lunch
___ 5. a mousetrap (something)	e. does not have an engine
___ 6. an ATM (machine)	f. "sees" with its ears
___ 7. a hurricane (a storm)	g. catches mice
___ 8. brunch (a meal)	h. stores energy

BELIEVE IT OR NOT

5 Beliefs

Work with a partner and take turns. Science has changed many of our beliefs. Each of you has a list of several beliefs that modern science has disproved or challenged. Read one of the past beliefs to your partner, starting the sentence with "People used to believe that . . ." Your partner should then state the modern belief.

EXAMPLE

Belief: Tomatoes are poisonous.

A: *People used to believe that tomatoes were poisonous.*

B: *Now we know that tomatoes are nutritious—although the leaves of the tomato plant are poisonous.*

Student A's statements are on page 250. Student B's statements are on page 256.

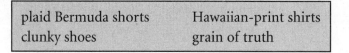

6 LISTENING: *"Stereotypes"*

A. Before you listen, make sure you understand this vocabulary:

plaid Bermuda shorts	Hawaiian-print shirts
clunky shoes	grain of truth

B. Listen to the recording. It begins and ends with some stereotypes about Americans. Write down as many of them as you can.

C. In small groups, discuss the stereotypes mentioned. Can you add any others? What is the "grain of truth" in these stereotypes? What makes them false? What stereotypes do people from other countries have about your country? Use expressions like:

People say that . . .
It's true that . . .
It isn't true that . . .

First listen to:

- Exercises 1 and 2.

Now record them.

Most cultures and societies have a creation myth or belief—a story about how the world or their nation was created. Talk for one minute and describe your culture's creation myth. Use sentences with *think that . . . , believe that . . .*, etc.

UNIT 42 Contractions and reductions of verbs

INTRODUCTION

➤ CONTRACTIONS OF VERBS

Use contractions after pronouns when you speak. Full forms sound formal in speaking; contractions sound more natural and friendly.

➤ REDUCTIONS OF VERBS

After nouns ending in consonants, auxiliary verbs are often reduced. Reductions join closely to the surrounding words. If this is difficult for you, use unreduced forms. Look at these common reductions.

Has, Is	
Has and *is* after [s, z, ʃ, ʒ, tʃ, dʒ] are reduced to [əz]. They sound like the "long plural" ending. Liz is athletic. "Lizzəz" Liz has started college. "Lizzəz"	
Have	
Have is reduced to [əv]. It sounds like *of.* The men have left. "men of/menəv"	
Had/Would	
Had and *would* are reduced to [əd]. They sound like the "long" past tense ending. Ann had seen the movie. "Annəd" Dominick would rather sleep. "Dominickəd"	
Will	***Are***
Will is reduced to [əl]. It sounds like an *-al* ending. The fine will be high. "final"	*Are* sounds like an *-er* ending. Where are my gloves? "wearer"

➤ CONTRACTIONS OF *NOT*

When you use the negative contraction *n't,* the auxiliary verb is stressed. **He ísn't in now.** **I dón't know that man.**
There is no contraction of *am* and *n't.* In tag questions, where a contraction is required, speakers use *aren't.* **I'm right, áren't I?**

➤ FAST SPEECH REDUCTIONS OF *DID*

The contractions and reductions described above are used in all styles of spoken English. You should also be aware of some fast speech reductions of *did.*

Listen to the reductions.

1. did + you	
What did you do?	**"Whaddidjə do"?**
Where did you go?	**"Wherejə go?"**
2. Question word + *did* + *he*	
When did he go?	**"Wendy go?"**
Who did he see?	**"Huwdiy see?"**
3. Question word + *did* + *her*	
Where did her husband go to school?	**"Wherdər" husband go to school**
Why did her roommate call?	**"Wider" roommate call**

➤ HIGHLIGHTING AUXILIARY VERBS

Stress auxiliary verbs when you need to highlight them—to emphasize their meaning, to show agreement, or to correct a statement.

A: The weather's horrible.
B: It IS horrible.

A: You haven't finished your paper yet.
B: I HAVE finished it. I'm just checking.

FOCUSED PRACTICE

1 DIALOGUES

First, read the dialogues and fill in the blanks with logical auxiliary verbs. Then listen to the dialogues to check your answers. Practice the dialogues with a partner. Use contractions and reductions and speak smoothly.

1. **A:** ____________ you ever used an online dating service?

   B: Never, but you know—I ____________ ____________ thinking about it.

   A: I ____________ checked some out and they seem pretty safe.

   B: So ____________ I. But you have to send in a picture. I ____________ be embarrassed if anyone I know ever saw my picture.

2. **A:** Who ____________ you go out with last night? Your roommate said you ____________ gone out.

   B: Yeah. A girl from school. She ____________ in a different class.

   A: So who is she? Do I know her?

   B: I don't know. I ____________ meeting her here now. Stick around and I ____________ introduce you.

2 HEARING REDUCTIONS

Listen to the sentences and repeat them. The underlined words have the same or nearly the same pronunciation. Then practice the sentences with a partner.

1. My watch is broken. Who fixes watches around here?
2. Their tenants have joined the tenants of the next building in a rent strike.
3. Your objection is logical, but I don't know if logic will convince them.

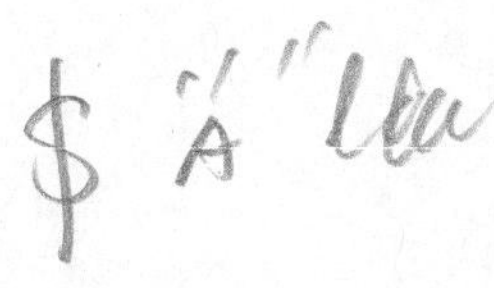

4. The ad had cost $800, which added to our total costs.
5. Some have spent some of the profits.
6. Why are there wires sticking out of the wall?
7. Why don't you chew more slowly?
8. Ed had edited it.

3 SOUNDS LIKE . . .

Two phrases that sound the same (or nearly the same) but have different spellings and meanings are called *homophrases.* Listen to these homophrases and repeat them. Then work with a partner to think of a homophrase that includes a reduced auxiliary verb. (Hint: An *-es* ending could be *has* or *is; of* could be *have;* an *-er* ending could be *are;* an *-al* ending could be *will.*) (You can check your answers on page 244.)

1. Alaska hunter *I'll ask a hunter.*
2. Roses scent the letter. Rose has send the letter
3. the Indians of Painted Towers ______
4. Answer fast. ______
5. The prizes cost a lot. ______
6. the seasonal change ______
7. summer home ______

LOVE IS IN THE AIR

4 CYBER ROMANCE

A. Listen to the recording and fill in the blanks.

Online dating services ______ proliferated on the Web. For people who have difficulty meeting other people, online services offer a private, relatively safe way ______ meet other people ______ find out about them before going on a date. The services provide a way ______ take some of the "blind" out of "blind dates." But ______ the people who use these services people you ______ like to go out with?

B. Discuss these questions with your partner:

1. Why do you think people use online dating services?
2. Have you ever used an online dating service? Would you? Why or why not?

5 Are They a Match?

Polly and Wayne have both listed themselves on an online dating service.

A. Before you listen, make sure you understand this vocabulary:

slim	down-to-earth	pubs
nice guys/naughty guys	wimps	wry (humor)
Aries	weight-train	martial arts

B. Listen to the recording and fill in the missing information for Polly and Wayne.

Polly	Wayne
Age ____ Height ______ Body Type ______	Age ____ Height ______ Body Type ______
Occupation ______________________	Occupation ______________________
Single ___ Divorced ___ Married ___ Children ___	Single ___ Divorced ___ Married ___ Children ___
Education ______________________	Education ______________________
Other	Other

C. In small groups, compare the charts for Polly and Wayne. What do they have in common? Do you think they'd like to go out with each other? Why or why not? What other information would *you* like to know about a person?

First listen to:

- Exercise 2.

Now record it.

Record a one-minute description of yourself. Include information similar to the information in the chart in Exercise 5. Speak smoothly and use contractions/reductions of auxiliary verbs.

UNIT 43

Reduction of modal perfects Reduction of "H-words"

INTRODUCTION

➤ MODAL PERFECTS: MODAL + *HAVE* + PAST PARTICIPLE

The auxiliary *have* is reduced to [əv] or [ə] and pronounced like an ending on the preceding word.

That might have happened. "mightəv"

That couldn't have happened. "couldəntəv"

You should have done it. "shoulddə done"

➤ H-WORD REDUCTIONS

Inside a sentence, the beginning *h* of personal pronouns and auxiliary verbs is often dropped. When *h* is dropped, the pronoun or verb joins closely to the preceding word. If it is difficult for you to join words together, you can pronounce the [h].

If he comes, give him the message. "iffy" "givim"

The bus had already left. "bussəd"

Pronounce *h* when there is a pause before the word, when the word needs to be highlighted, in short answers, and in *hasn't, haven't,* and *hadn't.*

He's réady. Wé don't care but hé does. Yes, I háve.

➤ *HAVE* AS A MAIN VERB

When *have, has,* or *had* is the main verb, *h* is usually not dropped. The vowel is not reduced to [ə].

She had a cold. [hǽd]

I'm having a hard time. [hǽvɪŋ]

FOCUSED PRACTICE

1 Modal Perfects

Listen to the sentences and repeat them. Reduce *have* and join it to the preceding word. Then practice the sentences with a partner.

1. Oh, I'm sorry. I should have been watching where I was going.
2. Don't worry. We can take it back. I should have asked you first.
3. I should have left earlier. I don't know when the next bus will come.
4. I guess I should have checked a cookbook first.
5. I know I should have done this last night, but I was just too busy.
6. Now I'll have to call a locksmith. I should have checked my bag before I left.
7. I should have listened to you and checked the tires at the gas station.
8. Another four pounds. I shouldn't have had so much.

2 Guesses with Modal Perfects

Work with a partner and make guesses about why the sentences in Exercise 1 were said. Use the modal perfects in the box and reduce *have.*

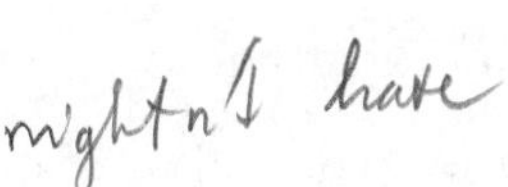

Strong guesses (99% sure)	*must (not) have* + Past Participle
Guesses	*might (not) have* + Past Participle *could have* + Past Participle
Impossible	*couldn't have* + Past Participle
Advice	*should(n't) have* + Past Participle

EXAMPLE

I knew I shouldn't have tried to go through that yellow light.

The person might have been speeding.

A policeman might have given him or her a ticket.

3 DIALOGUE

Listen to the dialogue. Cross out *h* in the underlined words if it is not pronounced. Then practice the dialogue with a partner. Speak smoothly.

A: Something's going on at the office with my boss. He isn't interested in what I have to say.

B: Maybe something's on his mind. Maybe it isn't you. Maybe it's him. Why don't you ask Rachel? She always has her ear to the ground.*

A: Yeah, I can trust her. I probably should have talked with her before now. The atmosphere's been different for a while.

B: Is your job in danger? Has your boss complained about your work?

A: He hasn't, but I know the manager in the sales department doesn't like me. He always gives me dirty looks.

B: Talk to Rachel. She might have heard something. In the meantime, maybe you'd better dust off your resume.

**ear to the ground:* knows what's going on

4 TWENTY QUESTIONS

A. Listen to the questions and repeat them.

1. Is he alive or dead?
2. What does he do?
3. What's her occupation?
4. How old is he?

B. Play the game Twenty Questions in small groups. Player One thinks of a person and gives the group the first letter of the person's name (for example, E for Albert Einstein). The other players can ask up to twenty questions (total, not per player) to find out who the person is. The player who guesses the person correctly then becomes Player One.

EXAMPLE

Player One: I'm thinking of a person whose last name begins with *P.*

A: Is the person male or female?

Player One: He's male.

B: Is he alive or dead?

THE TUNGUS EXPLOSION

5 LISTENING: *"What Happened in Tungus?"*

A. Listen to the passage about the Tungus explosion and fill in the blanks. Compare your answers with a partner. Listen again if you need to.

(1) In 1908 something very strange happened in Siberia. (2) At 7:17 A.M. on June 30, 1908, a powerful explosion occurred ____________ the air ____________ the forested Tungus area of Central Siberia. (3) The explosion ____________ so strong that it knocked down all the trees in a 20-mile radius from its center.

(4) A farmer ____________ sitting on the steps ____________ ____________ house about 40 miles from the explosion when ____________ saw a huge flash of light. (5) He looked away but immediately felt the ____________. (6) He said, "My shirt ____________ almost burned ____________ my body." (7) Then the force of the explosion hit ____________ and threw ____________ from the steps. (8) A neighbor's storage hut ____________ completely burned from the heat of the explosion, and all of ____________ metal tools ____________ melted.

(9) What ____________ ____________ produced such a strong explosion? (10) Several very different explanations ____________ ____________ proposed by people who ____________ studied this event. (11) Still, to this day no one is sure what ____________ ____________ caused the explosion over Siberia in 1908.

B. Work in small groups and compare your answers. Cross out unpronounced *h*'s. Do a group reading of the passage with each student reading a sentence. Then think of some possible explanations for the Tungus explosion. Use modal perfects. (You can check the answer key on page 244 for some explanations.)

____

____

____

____

____

First listen to:

- Exercise 1.

Now record it.

Think of something you did in the past that you now regret. Record what happened and why you now regret it. Use modal perfects to express what you should have done, could have done, etc.

PART 5

INTONATION

UNIT 44 Intonation overview

INTRODUCTION

Intonation is the melody of language. It refers to the patterning of high and low notes over sentences and phrases. The terms "intonation" and "pitch" sometimes mean the same thing; more often, "intonation" refers to the melody of sentences and phrases, while "pitch" refers to the note on a particular syllable.

This unit presents an overview of the pitch range of English, the use of intonation to highlight important information, common intonation patterns, and the use of intonation to express feelings and attitudes. Specific topics are presented in more detail in subsequent units.

PITCH RANGE IN ENGLISH

English is described as a three-toned ("note") language. A common intonation pattern is one that starts on a mid level, rises to a high pitch (note), and then falls to a low pitch.

There's a stranger at the door.

Speakers also use a fourth level of pitch, a very high note, for emphasis.

Be careful! There's a truck coming!

Some languages, like Japanese, Spanish, or Dutch, typically use a narrower range of pitch than English. Japanese and Spanish, for example, are described as two-toned languages. Native speakers of these languages may need to expand their pitch range to avoid sounding "flat" in English. On the other hand, native speakers of languages like Norwegian may need to use less variation in pitch when they speak English.

HIGHLIGHTING

There is usually one word in a sentence that is most important. This word is highlighted by using heavy stress, an extra-long vowel, and high pitch. Highlighting directs the listener's attention to the most important part of the sentence. Highlighted words are often words that present new information, a contrast, or a correction.

I DIALOGUES

Work with a partner. The questions in column A are asking for specific information. In column B, the words in capital letters highlight specific information. Listen to the sentences in column B. Match the questions in column A with responses in column B to create short dialogues. Then practice the dialogues. Use high pitch to highlight words.

A	B
____ **1.** What did you say? To the football game?	**a.** I want to go to the baseball GAME tomorrow.
____ **2.** Who wants to go?	**b.** I WANT to go to the baseball game tomorrow.
____ **3.** Today, did you say?	**c.** I want to go to the BASEBALL game tomorrow.
____ **4.** Do you have to go to the game?	**d.** I want to go to the baseball game TOMORROW.
____ **5.** What did you say? To the practice?	**e.** **I** want to go to the baseball game tomorrow.

SOME COMMON INTONATION PATTERNS

➤ FINAL FALLING INTONATION

The voice rises on the highlighted word and then falls to a low pitch to end the sentence. Final falling intonation is used when the speaker believes what (s)he is saying is a fact. Use this pattern with statements and information questions.

A: What did the weather report say?

B: It's going to rain.

➤ FINAL RISING INTONATION

The voice rises on the highlighted word and stays high or continues to rise to the end of the sentence. Final rising intonation indicates uncertainty. Use this pattern with *Yes/No* questions.

Is it raining yet?

2 HEARING INTONATION

Listen to the sentences. If intonation rises at the end of the sentence, put a question mark and a rising intonation line (↗) in the blank. If intonation falls at the end of the sentence, put a period and a falling intonation line (↘) in the blank.

1. Your car needs new tires.↘
2. Classes have been cancelled for today___
3. Felipe's going to Florida for Spring Break___
4. Spring Break's in mid-March___
5. Robert's never skied before___
6. Yuko and Nori went to Washington, D.C., last weekend___
7. They ran out of gas on the highway___

USING INTONATION TO EXPRESS FEELINGS AND ATTITUDES

Intonation tells the listener a great deal about a speaker's attitudes and feelings.

Listen to these examples:

	Intonation	Interpretation
1. Spring Break is a month away.	flat, mid-level pitch	bored, uninterested
2. Spring Break is a month away.	varied pitch	excited, interested
3. Spring Break is a month away.	Very high pitch on one word, with a continuing rise	surprise, disbelief
4. Spring Break is a month away.	low pitch, slow, heavy stress	controlled anger
5. Spring Break is a month away.	exaggerated pitch and length	sarcasm

3 Dialogues

Listen to the dialogues. Then practice them with a partner.

1. **Jaime:** What are you doing for Spring Break?
   Carol: I'm going skiing with Susana and Steve. What about you?
   Jaime: I don't have plans yet. I might go somewhere or I might just stay here.
   Carol: Well, at least you won't have classes.

2. **Rachel:** I think I need a break from Spring Break. I'm exhausted!
   John: Did you have a good time? You didn't call, so I expect you did.
   Rachel: It was great. You know—a lot of parties, dancing, music, food.
   John: I had a pretty good time here. I saw Peter and Melanie a couple of times. It was OK.

4 Interpreting Intonation

A. Listen to the sentences and circle the word that best describes the speaker's feeling.

1. I went to Florida last year for Spring Break.	bored	excited	angry
2. The beach was so crowded.	pleased	displeased	surprised
3. We spent every day in the sun.	sarcastic	pleased	angry
4. Six kids stayed in a motel room.	excited	angry	surprised
5. The flight back to Boston was delayed.	bored	angry	surprised
6. There was a lot of snow on the ground.	angry	pleased	surprised

B. Practice saying the sentences with a partner choosing different attitudes. Use your voice appropriately to express that attitude.

UNIT 45 Pitch range Intonation groups Final intonation patterns

INTRODUCTION

➤ INTONATION GROUPS

Intonation groups correspond to thought groups. They refer to the intonation or pitch pattern (contour) over a group of words. An intonation group usually includes a stressed word with higher pitch than other words in the thought group.

I'm tíred and my féet húrt.

In this sentence, there are two intonation groups, corresponding to the two thought groups. Pitch rises on *tired,* the stressed word in the first thought group, and again on *feet,* the highlighted word of the sentence. After *feet,* intonation falls to a low note to end the sentence.

➤ FINAL INTONATION PATTERNS

Final intonation patterns are intonation patterns that end sentences.

Final (Rising-) Falling Intonation

Pattern: Intonation rises on the highlighted word (the most important word of the sentence) and then falls to a low pitch to end the sentence.

It's hót in hére.

Sentence types: Statements, Information questions

Meaning: The final falling pattern indicates that the speaker is certain about what she has said. This pattern also shows that the speaker has finished speaking.

There's a letter for you.

A: What did you do this weekend?

B: Nothing.

Final Rising Intonation

Pattern: Intonation rises on the highlighted word and stays high or continues to rise to the end of the sentence.

Sentence types: *Yes/No* questions

Meaning: Final rising intonation indicates uncertainty. It can also show that the speaker has not finished speaking, although the voice does not rise as high as at the end of a *Yes/No* question.

Are you staying?

OK?

I think . . . (The speaker hasn't finished the sentence.)

FOCUSED PRACTICE

1 DIALOGUE

Listen to the dialogue and repeat it. Follow the intonation lines. Exaggerate high and low pitch. Then practice the dialogue with a partner.

A: What's the matter? What are you holding?

B: Nothing. It's just my VISA bill.

A: Is it high? Did you charge a lot of stuff?

B: Yeah, but this much? There must be a mistake!
I'm sure I didn't buy all these things.

A: Maybe it's fraud. Maybe somebody got your number and used it.

B: Maybe. . . . But all these stores are places I shop. Take a look.

A: This is three pages long! And look at the balance.

B: I can't even make the minimum payment!

2 Conversations of Questions

One way to avoid answering a question is to ask another question yourself. Listen to the dialogues and repeat them, using rising intonation. Then practice the dialogues with a partner.

1. **A:** Do you want to come?
   B: Do you want me to?
   A: If I say no, will you be angry?
   B: Do you care if I'm angry?

2. **A:** Does Boris live here?
   B: Are you a friend of his?
   A: Is this his house?
   B: Is he expecting you?

3. **A:** Did you find a brown wallet?
   B: Did you lose one?
   A: Isn't that a wallet over there?
   B: Do you have any identification?

3 Hearing Intonation

A. Listen to the sentences. If the speaker sounds certain, put a period (.) after the sentence and a falling intonation line (↘) in the blank. If the sentence sounds like a question, put a question mark after the sentence and a rising intonation line (↗) in the blank.

1. The midterm is next week? ↗
2. They're predicting a snowstorm for tomorrow___
3. Your credit card company increased your credit line___
4. The aerobics class is full now___
5. Maurice was a victim of credit card fraud___
6. Robert's car is at the mechanic's again___
7. Martha's going to be moving to Florida___
8. She's moving out at the end of the month___

B. Work with a partner. Read a sentence to your partner, using final falling or final rising intonation. Exaggerate the intonation so your partner can tell you whether you're stating a fact or asking a question.

4 CREDIT CARD TRIVIA

A. What do you know about credit card use in the United States? Take the quiz below. You can guess if you don't know the answer.

1. In 2001, nearly 1.5 million Americans filed for bankruptcy. Compared with 2000, this was
   a. a 40 percent increase.
   b. a 3 percent decrease.
   c. a 19 percent increase.
   d. a 4 percent increase.

2. In 2001, how much credit card debt did the average U.S. household have?
   a. $478 **c.** $1,069
   b. $5,477 **d.** $8,523

3. How many credit cards does the average American have?
   a. two **c.** about three
   b. about six **d.** one

4. How many Americans pay their credit cards off in full every month?
   a. 42 percent **c.** 15 percent
   b. 76 percent **d.** 33 percent

5. Assume you charge a $400 coat. The interest on your credit card is 18 percent and you make only the minimum payments. How long will it take you to pay off the coat?
   a. 2.1 years **c.** 3.6 years
   b. 13 months **d.** 5.2 years

B. Take turns asking and answering the poll questions with your partner. When you answer, use falling intonation if you're sure about your answer. If you aren't sure, use rising intonation. (When you finish, you can check your answers on page 244.) Then discuss these questions: Do you think credit card use is a problem? Why? Do people in your country use credit cards a lot?

5 INTERVIEWS

A. Interview two students about their spending habits and complete the chart on the next page.

continued

	Name ______	Name ______
Do you use credit cards?		
Questions for credit card users		
1. What kind of payments do you make?		
a. pay in full every month		
b. pay the minimum		
c. pay more than the minimum but not in full		
2. How many cards do you have?		
3. What type of things do you typically charge?		
Questions for credit card non-users		
1. How do you usually pay for things?		
a. with cash		
b. with a debit card		
c. with checks		
d. with money orders		

B. In a small group, discuss the results of your interviews: Do most students use credit cards? Do they have credit card debt? What do they charge with their cards?

First listen to:

- Exercise 1.

Now record it. Use intonation correctly and make sure your pitch varies.

Then record answers to these questions:

Why do you think so many people are deep in credit card debt?

Describe your own use of credit cards.

Do you think your spending habits are a problem?

UNIT 46 Listing intonation Rising intonation on question words

INTRODUCTION

➤ LISTING INTONATION

Words in a list are pronounced with listing intonation: The words before the last word of the list are pronounced with rising intonation. On the last word, intonation falls.

one, two, three

ambitious, intelligent, and energetic

➤ INTONATION PATTERNS WITH *OR*

Choice Questions with *or*. Choice questions ask the listener to choose an alternative. These questions are not answered with "yes" or "no."

Use listing intonation on the words joined by *or;* the choices are usually in different thought groups.

A: Do you want this one or that one?

B: That one.

A: Should I use a pencil or a pen?

B: A pen.

Open-Choice Questions. In some choice questions, the last choice is pronounced with rising pitch to show that the list is not complete: There may be other choices the speaker does not say.

What shall we have for dinner? Do you want fish, chicken, meat, . . . ?

Where shall we go for vacation? To Europe, Canada, Mexico . . . ?

continued

***Yes/No* Questions with *or*. Some questions with *or* do not present alternatives: They are true *Yes/No* questions and are pronounced with a final rising intonation. The words joined by *or* are grouped together.**

Do you want to go on Friday or Saturday? (It doesn't matter which day.)

Do you have a cat or dog? (It doesn't matter which.)

➤ QUESTION WORDS AND RISING INTONATION

Rising intonation on a question word can mean the speaker didn't hear what was said and is asking for a repetition. Falling intonation on the question word means that the speaker understood, but wants more information.

A: I've got something for you.

B: What?

A: I said, I've got something for you.

B: What?

A: Tickets to the concert.

FOCUSED PRACTICE

1 DIALOGUES

Listen to the dialogues and repeat them. Then practice the dialogues with a partner.

1. **A:** Are you ready to order?

   B: Yes. I'll have coffee, a corn muffin, and orange juice.

2. **A:** What are the Columbia, the Missouri, and the Mississippi?

   B: They're the three largest rivers in the United States.

3. **A:** When you were in Seattle, did you see the Space Needle or the Pike Place Market?

   B: No. I just visited the university and went shopping.

4. **A:** What would you like: a one-bedroom, a studio, a view, close to transportation?

B: I want a studio that's close to the university, quiet, and furnished.

2 Intonation with Question Words

Listen to the dialogue and repeat it. Draw intonation lines (↗ or ↘) to show the intonation on the question words. Then practice the dialogue with a partner.

A: I heard some good gossip.

B: What?

A: I said I heard some good gossip.

B: What?

A: Maria and Tony are getting married soon.

B: When?

A: Soon. I said soon.

B: When?

A: I think next month.

3 Complete the Dialogue

Work with a partner and complete the dialogues. Each dialogue can be completed in two ways, depending on whether the question word is asking for a repetition or for more information. If you are reading B's part, exaggerate the intonation on the question word so your partner knows whether you want a repetition or more information.

1. **A:** I heard some interesting news.

   B: What?

   A: ______________________________

2. **A:** I met someone nice today.

   B: Who?

   A: ______________________________

continued

3. **A:** My mother will be arriving next week.

   B: When?

   A: ______________________________

4. **A:** We're going to meet at a restaurant after class.

   B: Where?

   A: ______________________________

4 JEOPARDY

Jeopardy is a game where the answers are known and you have to think of the questions.

Play this game in pairs. You and your partner will take turns being the *host* (the one who has the information) and the *contestant* (the one who must provide information).

Here's how to play:

- **Contestant:** Choose an amount (100, 200, 300, 400, 500) to risk in one of the categories. The higher the amount, the greater the difficulty.
- **Host:** Read the information (the answer) for that amount. Since there are three pieces of information, use listing intonation.
- **Contestant:** Say a question that makes sense for the answer the host just read, using falling intonation with the question. If you don't understand the host, ask *What?*, using rising intonation to show you want a repetition.
- If the question is correct, the contestant earns the amount assigned to that answer. If the question is incorrect, the contestant loses that amount.

EXAMPLE

A: I'll take Bodies of Water for 100 points.

B: the Mississippi, the Amazon, and the Thames

A: What?

B: the Mississippi, the Amazon, and the Thames

A: What are rivers?

B: That's correct for 100 points!

Student A's answers are on page 250. Student B's answers are on page 256.

5 CHOOSING A PLACE TO LIVE

A. What criteria are important when you choose a place to live? Read the list below and check the three factors that would most influence your decision to rent/buy a particular house or apartment.

Price	___	Size/space	___
Neighborhood	___	Parking	___
Noise level	___	Location (close to school/ work/shopping)	___
Sunlight	___	Other	___
Furnished	___		

B. In a small group, share your criteria, using listing intonation. Do you all agree on what criteria are important? Does the place you're living in now meet your criteria?

First listen to:

- Exercise 1.

Now record it.

Review the criteria for choosing a place to live in Exercise 5. Which three criteria are most important to you? Least important? Explain why. Pay attention to intonation.

UNIT 47 Tag questions Drop-rise intonation

INTRODUCTION

Tag questions are questions like *didn't you?* that are added to the ends of sentences. You can use rising or falling intonation on a tag question.

You sent the letter, didn't you? He can't dance, can he?

➤ USE RISING INTONATION ON TAG QUESTIONS

To Change a Statement into a True Question: The speaker doesn't know the answer to the question.

I paid that money back to you, didn't I? I hope I didn't forget.

I think I've heard him play before. He's a jazz musician, isn't he?

To Make a Command More Polite:

Bring that here, would you? **Open that window, won't you?**

➤ USE FALLING INTONATION ON TAG QUESTIONS

When You Think the Sentence Is True: Falling intonation shows you expect confirmation.

Look at those clouds. It's going to rain, isn't it?

Another price increase. Well, prices never go down, do they?

To Indicate Sarcasm: The intonation is exaggerated.

He's such a *nice* man, isn't he? (meaning: He isn't nice.)

To Show Agreement with a Previous Statement: Tag questions are used alone with falling intonation and usually don't end in a question mark.

A: It's awfully cold today.

B: Isn't it.

➤ DROP-RISE INTONATION WITH *YES/NO* QUESTIONS

The drop-rise intonation pattern is polite and somewhat formal. It is often used with strangers to ask for help or information. Intonation drops quickly on the highlighted word to a low pitch and then rises again. Listen.

Do you have the time?   Where can I make a phone call?

FOCUSED PRACTICE

1 Hearing Intonation

Listen to the sentences. Draw the intonation over the tag questions (╲ or ╱).

1. It's time to go, isn't it?
2. You forgot your keys again, didn't you?
3. You can help me tonight, can't you?
4. You're not leaving so soon, are you?
5. They don't have the money, do they?
6. The bus hasn't left yet, has it?

2 Complete the Dialogues

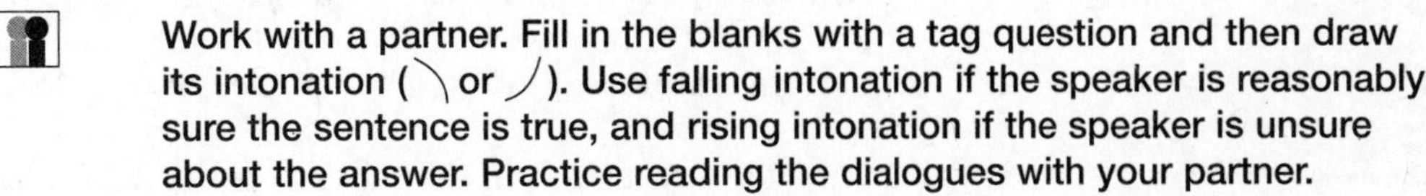

Work with a partner. Fill in the blanks with a tag question and then draw its intonation (╲ or ╱). Use falling intonation if the speaker is reasonably sure the sentence is true, and rising intonation if the speaker is unsure about the answer. Practice reading the dialogues with your partner.

1. (A and B have just been introduced at X's party.)

   A: This is a nice party, ______________?

   B: Yes—X always gives great parties.

2. **A:** Honey, I'm afraid I've got some bad news.

   B: You haven't lost your job, ______________?

3. **A:** Honey, I've got great news!

   B: I know what it is—you got that promotion, ______________?

4. **A:** This was a great dinner. Thank you.

   B: Have some more cake, ______________?

3 AGREEING

Work with a partner. Complete the dialogues by writing "agreement" tag questions in the blanks. Then practice the dialogues. Use falling intonation on the tag question.

1. **A:** The snow looks so dirty after it's been on the ground for a few days.
   B: *Doesn't it.*
2. **A:** The midterm was really easy.
   B: ____________________
3. **A:** There were a lot of people at the New Students' Reception.
   B: ____________________
4. **A:** It's been a long time since we last talked.
   B: ____________________

4 DROP-RISE INTONATION

Listen to the sentences and repeat them. Which word does the intonation drop on? Circle the word. Then practice the questions with a partner.

1. Excuse me. Where is the (admission's) office?
2. (to a stranger in a bus) Is this seat taken?
3. (to a stranger) I can't open this—could you give me a hand?
4. (to an airline employee) When is the plane going to leave?
5. (to a stranger next to you in the theater) Is this your coat?

JUST THE FACTS

5 GUESSING INFORMATION

A. Without asking your partner, fill out the chart about him or her. If you don't know the answer, make a guess. Write something in each blank.

Full name ____________________

Address ____________________

Occupation ____________________

Date of birth ______________________________

Marital status ______________________________

Children ______________________________

Citizenship ______________________________

Native language ______________________________

Reason for studying English ______________________________

Favorite type of music ______________________________

Favorite TV show ______________________________

Favorite color ______________________________

B. Now tell your partner what you wrote, using full sentences that end with a tag question. If you're reasonably sure the information for an item is correct, use falling intonation on the tag question. If you are not sure, use rising intonation. Correct the information that is wrong.

EXAMPLE

Your full name is Felix Ungar, isn't it?

First listen to:

- Exercise 1.

Now record it. Pay attention to intonation.

Write four sentences ending with tag questions about these celebrities. Your sentences should give information about the people. If you're not sure about the information, use rising intonation on the tag. If you're sure, use falling intonation.

Tom Cruise   Nicole Kidman

UNIT 48 Nonfinal intonation

INTRODUCTION

➤ NONFINAL INTONATION CHANGES

Intonation rises (or falls) slightly at the end of a clause or thought group, but it does not change as much as it does at the end of a sentence. Nonfinal intonation changes help mark the parts of the sentence for the listener.

I'll come as soon as possible. I'll do it if I can.

➤ UNFINISHED SENTENCES

Sometimes speakers pause before they've finished speaking. To show that your sentence is unfinished, don't let your intonation drop when you pause.

Turn left at the corner . . . then go straight for five blocks.

FOCUSED PRACTICE

1 DIFFERENCES IN MEANING

A. The way in which words are grouped and pronounced together can affect meaning. Listen to the sentences in the first column and repeat them. Use intonation and thought groups to show how the words are grouped together. Then listen again and circle the meaning that matches the sentence you hear.

Sentences	Meaning
1. a. My brother, who won the lottery, finally got married.	I have one brother.
b. My brother who won the lottery finally got married.	I have more than one brother.
2. a. "Joe," replied Sam, "is my best friend."	Sam said Joe was his best friend.
b. Joe replied, "Sam is my best friend."	Joe said Sam was his best friend.

	Sentences	Meaning
3.	**a.** I promised not to tell, Felipe.	I told Felipe I would not reveal something.
	b. I promised not to tell Felipe.	I said I would not tell Felipe.
4.	**a.** I have three, hundred-year-old coins.	I have three coins that are 100 years old.
	b. I have 300-year-old coins.	I have some coins that are 300-years old.
5.	**a.** The employees, who got pink slips,* were devastated.	All the employees got pink slips.
	b. The employees who got pink slips were devastated.	Some employees got pink slips.

**pink slip:* a notice that an employee has been laid off from work

B. Work with a partner and take turns. Choose a sentence from Part A and say it to your partner. Use intonation and thought groups when you speak so your partner can tell you which meaning you intended.

2 FINISH YOUR THOUGHT

A. Listen to the sentences. If the speaker is finished with the sentence, write "Finished" in the blank. If the speaker is not finished, write "Unfinished."

1. I'll start looking for another job *Finished*
2. Return the books to the library ____________
3. Alex thinks he's going to make a lot of money ____________
4. He left work early ____________
5. Make sure you bring your ID card ____________
6. Lee's boss doesn't ask him for suggestions ____________
7. My job became unbearable ____________
8. She used to be invited to make suggestions ____________

B. Work with a partner and take turns. Read a sentence to your partner. Use appropriate intonation so your partner can tell you whether you've finished speaking or plan to say more.

IT'S TIME TO GO

3 BREATH GROUPS

A. **Read this passage and underline thought groups. Then practice reading the passage with a partner. (You and your partner may have different thought groups.)**

In the old work model, employees exchanged job loyalty for job security. Today, that model is out-of-date in many areas of employment. Workers feel less loyalty to their employers, and employers provide less security to their workers. As a result, the chance that you will be employed by the same employer for your entire work life is getting smaller and smaller.

But changing jobs is difficult. Many employees wait until a work situation has become intolerable. Or, even worse, they may wait until they are forced to leave a job. Employees need to be able to recognize the signs that say it's time to look for another job.

B. **Listen to the recording. Take notes on the eight signs that it's time to look for another job.**

C. **Work with a partner. Use your notes to paraphrase the signs mentioned in the recording. Use intonation and thought groups to organize the parts of your sentences. Here are some sentence frames to help you paraphrase:**

If . . . , it may be time to go.

You should think about another job if/when . . .

4 INTERVIEWS

Interview two classmates about past and future jobs. Then share the information with the class.

	Name ______	Name ______
What jobs have you had?		
Why did you leave past jobs?		
How many jobs do you think you'll have in your life?		
In what fields do you want to work?		
Have you ever had two jobs at the same time?		
Do you think you'll continue to get training and education throughout your work life?		
Do most people in your country keep the same job their whole career?		

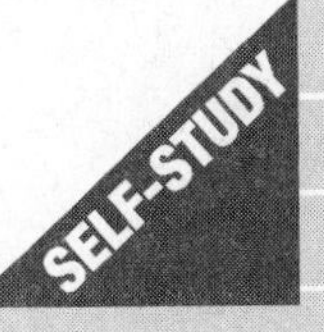

First listen to:

- Exercise 1.

Now record it.

Record your own answers to the questions in Exercise 4. Answer in complete sentences, and use thought groups and intonation to organize them.

UNIT 49 Expressive intonation

INTRODUCTION

➤ INTONATION AND MEANING

Intonation conveys meaning. It can change a question into a statement or focus the listener's attention on a specific word in the sentence.

➤ INTONATION AND FEELINGS

Your intonation also tells the listener how you feel: whether you are happy or angry, bored or surprised. When you speak English, it is important to use a wide range of pitch. If your intonation is flat, your listener may think you are bored.

Listen to the speaker say the phrase "Burgers again." Read the description of the intonation and its interpretation.

	Intonation	Interpretation
Burgers again	low, flat, heavy stress	controlled anger
Burgers again	varied pitch	pleasure
Burgers again	very extreme pitch, exaggerated length	sarcasm
Burgers again	very high, rising pitch	disbelief, surprise
Burgers again	mid-level pitch, flat, soft	boredom

FOCUSED PRACTICE

1 INTERPRETING INTONATION

Listen to the dialogues. Circle the word that best describes how B feels.

1. **A:** Your sister called this afternoon.

   B: What did she say?

   Bored Pleased Angry

2. **A:** The exam has been put off until next week.
   B: That's such good news.
   Pleased — Sarcastic — Bored

3. **A:** Carol is transferring to another school next semester.
   B: She is? I'll really miss her.
   Disappointed — Sarcastic — Bored

4. **A:** I'm giving my girlfriend tickets to the game for Christmas.
   B: She'll love that. You know how she loves basketball.
   Approving — Sarcastic — Angry

5. **A:** I think your English has improved a lot.
   B: I think yours has, too.
   Pleased — Angry — Bored

6. **A:** What do you think of this sweater?
   B: It's really cheap.
   Favorable opinion — Unfavorable opinion — Doesn't care

2 Telephone Call

A. Listen to the telephone conversation and repeat the lines. How does Max feel about the news that Sarah is selling their car?

Max Fremont: Hello?
Robert Morse: Hello. Is Sarah Fremont there?
M: No, she isn't. She's out for the day. May I take a message?
R: I'm calling about the car she's selling.
M: She's selling the car?
R: Uh, yeah. There's an ad in the paper. A '98 Chevy Cavalier.
M: And you're interested in buying that car.
R: Yeah. My name's Robert Morse and my number's 555-2784. Can you tell her I called?
M: I'll give her the message.

B. Practice the dialogue with a partner. Read Max's part in different ways: He doesn't care what happens to the car; he's glad the car's being sold; he's angry the car's being sold.

3 Disbelief

Listen to the dialogues and repeat the lines. B's responses show disbelief or denial of something A has said. Notice how the intonation starts high on the subject pronoun, falls, and then rises on the word that B believes is false. Practice the dialogues with a partner.

1. **A:** There's a great parking spot over there.

   B: You can't park there! That's a hydrant.

2. **A:** Let's stop for a minute at this pet store.

   B: You don't have a pet. Why do you want to stop there?

3. **A:** I want to buy something like that for my wife.

   B: You aren't married! What do you mean, your wife?

4. **A:** I'm taking Emily out dancing tonight.

   B: You don't know how to dance! Why are you doing that?

4 Escalation

Listen to the dialogues and repeat the lines. How does the intonation change as the dialogue progresses? Practice the dialogues with a partner. Use intonation to show how the mood in the dialogue changes.

1. The Hike

   A: This looks like an easy hike. I think we can do it.

   B: Oh, yeah. The trail's in good shape and the weather couldn't be better.

   A: What's this? What happened to the trail? Is this the trail?

   B: Don't ask me—this is your hike! Is that rain I feel?

   A: Forget the rain. How are we going to get up that?

   B: Up? Forget up! How are we going to get down? Easy hike!

2. Installing a Ceiling Light

   A: These instructions look easy. We can do this.

   B: Just get an electrician. Look at all the wires!

   A: Yeah, but there are instructions. You just read the instructions. I'll do the wiring.

B: I don't know about this. OK. It says match the black wire in the light to the black wire from the ceiling. Then white to white.

A: You're on the wrong page! There's nothing black or white here.

B: I'm on the ONLY page. This is your bright idea—you read the instructions. I'm making a sandwich.

5 Hearing Intonation

Listen to this dialogue. Draw arrows in the blanks to show the intonation on the question words. Then circle the meaning of the question word. Practice the dialogue with a partner.

Joe: Hi, Mary.

Mary: Hi.

Joe: Did you have a nice weekend?

Mary: What? ______ wants information didn't hear disbelief

Joe: I asked if you'd had a nice weekend.

Mary: Why? ______ wants information didn't hear disbelief

Joe: Why? ______ wants information didn't hear disbelief

Mary: I mean, why do you want to know?

Joe: Want to know what?

Mary: If I had a nice weekend. Why do you want to know?

Joe: Let's just forget the whole thing.

Mary: Forget what? ______ wants information didn't hear disbelief

Joe: What I asked you.

Mary: What did you ask me?

Joe: I've forgotten. . . . See you, Mary.

6 COURSES FOR MEN AND WOMEN

Here are some humorous courses that men and women would recommend for the opposite sex. The humor is based on stereotypes that men and women have of each other.

A. Work with a partner and take turns. Read the course titles to each other. How should you read them to show that they're jokes?

Cooking 101:	How Not to Force Your Diet on Others
Cooking 102:	Beyond Hot Dogs and Beer
Bathrooms 101:	How to Change a Roll of Toilet Paper
Bathrooms 102:	How to Shower in Five Minutes or Less
Driving 101:	Cars Need Both Gas AND Oil
Driving 102:	Introduction to Asking for Directions
Communication Skills 101:	Introduction to Hanging Up the Telephone
Communication Skills 102:	Pronunciation of "I Love You"
Classic Clothing 101:	Wearing Clothes You Already Have
Classic Clothing 102:	Just Because It's Comfortable Doesn't Mean It's Classic

B. With your partner, decide which courses women would recommend that men take, and which courses men would recommend that women take. What stereotypes of men and women do the course titles reflect?

First listen to:

- Exercise 1.

Now record it. Record each dialogue three times to reflect three different feelings (for example, bored, angry, and pleased).

Next, choose four of the course titles from Exercise 6. Read the course titles to show they are jokes. Then explain the stereotypes that the four courses reflect.

UNIT EXERCISE ANSWERS

UNIT 2

Exercise 7 Page 10

Good gifts and reasons: tickets to see his favorite sports team (she pays attention to his needs); a gift he can use for his favorite hobby (she wants him to enjoy himself); race-car driving lessons (she wants to add excitement to his life); a book from the best-seller list (she thinks he's intellectual); silver cufflinks (they're classy); a sweater (a symbol of style and warmth)

Bad gifts and reasons: opera tickets (it's a present for herself); a picture of her (she thinks too much of herself); ties (very "cliché"); electric razor (boring); tools (she wants him to do some work for her); white socks (she has no fashion sense—she doesn't care)

UNIT 5

Exercise 4 Page 23

2. announcement **3.** hostel, hostile **4.** status **5.** polluted **6.** banana **7.** command **8.** appearance **9.** tonight

UNIT 22

Exercise 4 Page 108

2. The vine'll die.
3. The cat'll run away.
4. Your logic'll persuade her.
5. I'll ask a fisherman.
6. The comic'll joke

UNIT 25

Exercise 4 Page 122

2. It falls through the cracks. (an idiom meaning "something that never gets done")
3. I was flipping the channels on the TV.
4. our dear old queen
5. lighting a fire
6. a crushing blow
7. brain damage
8. grilled cheese
9. sleepy time

Exercise 6 Part A, Page 123

1. True; researchers believe that adolescent boys and girls experience the same amount of stress, but they don't always react in the same way to the same stress trigger.
2. False; stress is more likely to result in depression in girls.
3. False; chronic problems with relationships result in long-term stress.
4. True.
5. True.
6. False; the body's response in acute stress situations may be positive: for example, acute stress may give people an advantage during sports contests, or at a presentation for an important meeting. The effects of persistent stress on the body are negative.
7. False; less educated people are more vulnerable to the effects of stress.
8. True.

UNIT 26

Exercise 5 Page 128

Rap: Eminem
Country: Garth Brooks
Latin pop: Enrique Iglesias
Heavy Metal: Def Leppard
Rock and roll: The Beatles
Jazz: Louis Armstrong
Reggae: Bob Marley
Opera: Placido Domingo
Classical: Yo Yo Ma

UNIT 33

Exercise 5 Page 163

2. Will he pick it?
3. Seen your class schedule?
4. the right or left
5. Save your stories.
6. They can serve water.
7. The dress is in the closet.
8. a noise

Exercise 6 Part A, Page 164

1. c **2.** a **3.** b **4.** b **5.** c **6.** c **7.** c **8.** a

UNIT 36

Exercise 2 Page 178

N: Palerider, (are) you there?
P: What's up?
N: (I) talked to Sue today. She likes you. Me, too.
P: I like you, too. Sue said she likes me?
N: Yes.
P: (I'm) working. (I've) got to go.
N: OK. (I'll) see you tomorrow.
P: (I'll) see you, too. Bye.
N: Bye.

UNIT 37

Exercise 3 Page 182

2. a rested suspect
3. a rival city
4. a tension
5. a parent reasons (here, *reason* is a verb)
6. an attractive style

UNIT 38

Exercise 3 Page 189

2. They explained these in credible terms.
3. That's a device of technology.
4. I don't believe in direct advice.
5. The legislation was passed by an act of Congress.

UNIT 40

Exercise 3 Page 197

2. f **3.** g **4.** h **5.** i **6.** e **7.** d **8.** b **9.** a

UNIT 42

Exercise 3 Page 208

2. Rose has sent the letter.
3. The Indians have painted towers.
4. Ants are fast.
5. The prize has cost a lot.
6. The season will change.
7. Some are home.

UNIT 43

Exercise 5 Part B, Page 213

1. Scientists first believed a huge meteorite must have fallen from the sky and exploded. However, if a meteorite had fallen, it should have left a deep hole in the ground—but this didn't happen.
2. In the 1950s, people suggested that a spaceship from an advanced civilization might have tried to land on earth. They believed that the spaceship must have had trouble and exploded in midair.
3. Some scientists believe that a comet might have entered the earth's atmosphere and exploded in midair. Other scientists disagree because a comet is very large and would have been noticed by many people.
4. The most recent explanation is that a very small black hole might have hit the earth, gone straight through the earth, and come out the other side in the North Atlantic.

UNIT 45

Exercise 4 Part A, Page 223

1. c **2.** d **3.** b **4.** a **5.** d

APPENDIX I: for team 1 players

UNIT 1

Exercise 5 Fill in the Grid

Do not show your partner your grid. Ask your partner questions to complete your grid: for example, "What's in box *A2*?" When you have both completed your grids, compare them. They should be the same.

	1	2	3	4
A	waiter			
B		wetter		
C		stuck	stock	
D	main	man	stack	men

UNIT 2

Exercise 5 Fill in the Grid

Do not show your partner your grid. Ask your partner questions to complete your grid: for example, "What's in box *A2*?" When you have both completed your grids, compare them. They should be the same.

	1	2	3	4
A	list			steal/steel
B			least	
C	still	better	rich	
D		bitter	reach	

UNIT 4

Exercise 2 The [æ]-[ɛ] Game

1. If you don't see well, you may need to wear these.
2. What's a word for a "short coat"?
3. What's a word for "money"?
4. What's the past tense of "say"?
5. What do you put in a car to make it go?
6. What's the opposite of "hell"?
7. You can take pictures with this.
8. Dogs and cats have fur covering their bodies. What do birds have?
9. What kind of food does McDonald's sell?
10. What's the opposite of "cheap"?

Answers:

1. glasses **2.** jacket **3.** cash **4.** said **5.** gas (gasoline) **6.** heaven **7.** camera **8.** feathers **9.** fast food/hamburgers/French fries/sandwiches **10.** expensive

UNIT 5

Exercise 6A Can't Buy Me Love

Read these statements to your partner. Your partner will decide which intangible money is being used to buy.

1. I really don't spend much money on anything. I save almost everything I make. You never know what's going to happen. What am I going to do with a bunch of nice clothes if I lose my job?
2. The clothes I wear, the car I drive, the neighborhood I live in—they're all important in my line of work. They're signs that I'm not just your average Joe. My clients want to know that—they don't want me to be average.
3. Our company contributed heavily to your election campaign, and we expect you to protect our interests in Congress by supporting legislation that doesn't hurt this company.

UNIT 6

Exercise 2 Fill in the Grid

Do not show your partner your grid. Ask your partner questions to complete your grid: for example, "What's in box *A2*?" When you both complete your grids, compare them. They should be the same.

	1	2	3	4
A	bucks			dock
B			box	
C	deck		nut	backs
D		not	duck	

UNIT 7

Exercise 6 Jeopardy: Firsts

Start as the host. When your partner selects an amount, read the clue for that amount. Your partner must guess the *question*. Pronounce *first* correctly.

100: This man was the first president of the United States in the twenty-first century.
200: According to the Bible, these were the first two people on earth.
300: This man is recognized as the first European to discover the New World.
400: This country was the first to win the World Cup four times.
500: This man was the first person to walk on the moon.
[Who was/is George W. Bush? Who were Adam and Eve? Who was Christopher Columbus? What is Brazil? Who was Neil Armstrong?]

Contestant role: Choose an amount: 100, 200, 300, 400, or 500. When your partner reads you the clue, say the *question* that the clue answers.

UNIT 10

Exercise 4 The [ɑy]-[aw]-[oy] Game

1. What's the name of a sweet frozen milk product usually eaten in summer?
2. What word describes a period of time that's not in the morning, not in the afternoon, not in the evening, but late at ___________?
3. How would you describe courses that you must take (they are not electives)?
4. What phrase describes someone who isn't late or early?
5. What's a synonym for "afraid"?
6. Your nose is in the middle of your face. Where are your ears?
7. What's the opposite of "inside"?
8. What's a two-syllable word that means "crash"?
9. What's the adjective for "width"?
10. What's a polite response to make when you meet someone new?

Answers:

1. ice cream **2.** night **3.** requirements/required courses **4.** on time **5.** frightened **6.** on the side/sides **7.** outside **8.** collide **9.** wide **10.** Nice to meet you./How do you do?

UNIT 11

Exercise 4 Fill in the Grid

Do not show your partner your grid. Ask your partner questions to complete your grid: for example, "What's in box *A3*?" When you both complete your grids, compare them. They should be the same.

	1	2	3	4
A	sing	thing		
B	past	fast		correct
C				collect
D	fourth	force		

UNIT 14

Exercise 4 The TH Game

1. In the American Civil War, which side won?
2. What's an adjective that means "two"?
3. What's the name of our planet?

4. What's an instrument that measures temperature?
5. What's 20 + 10?
6. What fraction do you get if you divide 1 by 1,000?
7. What's a word for the front of the neck?
8. What's the part of the news that tells you about rain or snow?
9. What's another word for a robber?
10. What's a word that describes what's between "everything" and "nothing"?
11. Life starts with ____________.
12. What's the sound of lightning?
13. These white things in your mouth help you chew.
14. If you're nervous, take a deep ____________.

Answers:

1. the North **2.** both **3.** the earth **4.** thermometer **5.** 30 **6.** (one) one-thousandth, a thousandth **7.** throat **8.** the weather (report) **9.** a thief **10.** something **11.** birth **12.** thunder **13.** teeth **14.** breath

UNIT 15

Exercise 5 Box Office Hits

Top-Grossing Movies Worldwide* (from release to 9/2002)			
Rank	**Title**	**Year released**	**Box office earnings**
1	*Titanic*	1997	$1,835,000,000**
2			
3	*Star Wars Episode 1—The Phantom Menace*	1999	$922,000,000
4			
5			
6			
7	*Spiderman*	2002	$804,000,000
8	*Star Wars*	1977	$798,000,000
9			
10	*E.T. the Extra-Terrestrial*	1982	$757,000,000

*Source: www.us.imdb.com, 9/17/02
**Say "one billion eight hundred thirty-five million dollars."

UNIT 19

Exercise 6A Arguing Styles

	You	Your partner
1. When your partner wants to argue, do you leave or find some way to avoid the argument?	Usually ☐ Sometimes ☐ Rarely ☐	Usually ☐ Sometimes ☐ Rarely ☐
2. If you hurt your partner's feelings in an argument, do you apologize?	Usually ☐ Sometimes ☐ Rarely ☐	Usually ☐ Sometimes ☐ Rarely ☐
3. Do you ask for your partner's side of the story when you argue?	Usually ☐ Sometimes ☐ Rarely ☐	Usually ☐ Sometimes ☐ Rarely ☐
4. When you argue, do you attack your partner where you know it will hurt?	Usually ☐ Sometimes ☐ Rarely ☐	Usually ☐ Sometimes ☐ Rarely ☐
5. Do you believe it's better to fight than to hold in negative feelings?	Usually ☐ Sometimes ☐ Rarely ☐	Usually ☐ Sometimes ☐ Rarely ☐
6. Do you end up fighting about something completely different from the problem you started with?	Usually ☐ Sometimes ☐ Rarely ☐	Usually ☐ Sometimes ☐ Rarely ☐
7. Do you view arguments as an opportunity for growth?	Usually ☐ Sometimes ☐ Rarely ☐	Usually ☐ Sometimes ☐ Rarely ☐
8. Do your arguments solve the problems you fight about?	Usually ☐ Sometimes ☐ Rarely ☐	Usually ☐ Sometimes ☐ Rarely ☐

UNIT 20

Exercise 6 Immigration Quiz

Ask your partner these questions. Your partner has the choices for each question. Give your partner information about both correct and incorrect answers.

1. What proportion of the total U.S. population in 1990 was born in another country?*
   a. 22.7 percent. Incorrect. This is the proportion for Australia; 22.7 percent of Australians were foreign-born in the 1990s.

b. 16 percent. Incorrect. This was the proportion for Canada; 16 percent of the Canadian population was foreign-born in the 1990s.

c. 8.5 percent. Correct (1990).

2. The total U.S. population in 2000 was 274,000,000. What was the number who were foreign-born?**

a. 38 million. Incorrect. This is the number projected for 2020.

b. 28 million. Correct (for the year 2000).

c. 55 million. Incorrect. This was the number of Americans in 1997 who were born in another country or had at least one parent born in another country.

*Information from the Cato Institute, www.cato.org
**Information from the U.S. Census Bureau, www.census.gov

Select from these answers when your partner asks you questions:

3. a. 45 percent	**b.** 26 percent	**c.** 22 percent
4. a. 34 percent	**b.** 26 percent	**c.** 15 percent

UNIT 21

Exercise 6 The Love Poll

	You	Your Partner	1999 Poll (%) Women	Men
1. Do you believe in love at first sight?				
a. Yes	____	____	49%	48%
b. No	____	____	49	49
c. Not sure	____	____	2	3
2. Being as honest as you can, are you more attracted to people because of their bodies or their brains/personalities?				
a. Bodies	____	____	24%	43%
b. Brains/ personalities	____	____	60	35
c. Both	____	____	10	17
d. Not sure	____	____	6	5
3. If you could have only one of the following, which would you pick?				
a. Money	____	____	5%	9%
b. Health	____	____	63	49
c. Love	____	____	30	39

UNIT 22

Exercise 5 Quotations with Dark L

Quote 1

a. a word that means the opposite of "wise"; a word that means "deceive" or "trick"; a word that rhymes with "tool"

b. a word that means everyone; a word that rhymes with "tall"

c. a word that means "men and women"; a more common way of saying "persons"

d. what the clock tells you; a word that rhymes with "lime"

e. the same as *c.*

f. the same as *b.*

g. the same as *a.*

h. the same as *b.*

i. the same as *c.*

j. the same as *b.*

Quote 2

a. another word for "little"; a word that rhymes with "tall"

b. not a woman but a ______; a word that rhymes with "tan"

c. a word that means "a large step"; a word that rhymes with "keep"

d. a man's first name that rhymes with "meal"; a word that sounds the same as the verb that means "be on your knees"

Answers:

Quote 1: **a.** fool **b.** all **c.** people **d.** time **e.** people **f.** all **g.** fool **h.** all **i.** people **j.** all

Quote 2: **a.** small **b.** man **c.** leap **d.** Neil

UNIT 29

Exercise 5 College Courses

Ask your partner questions to complete the transcript.

Fall 2002	Grade	Course description
Engl3972		
GenS2602		
Econ3015	C	Economics 3015. Urban economics. This course covers the theories of location and land rents; transportation and the pricing of transit systems; crime and the allocation of police services.
ArtH3042	B–	Art History 3042. The American City. This course presents a survey of urban design and city planning, focusing on four cities: New York, Chicago, Washington, D.C., and Los Angeles. It investigates the impact of railroads, the automobile, and skyscrapers on the physical form of cities.

UNIT 30

Exercise 4 Trivia

Ask your partner these questions. Your partner will guess the answers. Say "higher" or "lower" until your partner guesses the correct percentage.

1. What percent of people thought that Barbra Streisand was the best female singer of the twentieth century? (14%)
2. What percent of people felt that wars would be the most important problem of the twenty-first century? (18%)
3. What percent of people thought their quality of life would be better in 2020? (60%)
4. What percent of people felt the Internet would still be used by the end of the twenty-first century? (about 80%)
5. What percent of people felt that printed books would be out-of-date by the end of the twenty-first century? (about 30%)

Sources: **1.** Zogby International Reuters/Zogby Poll, April 5–7, 1999, 1,008 adults nationwide (United States); **2.** CBS News Poll, December 17–19, 1999, 1,026 adults nationwide (United States); **3.** The Harris Poll, November 11–15, 1998; 1,010 adults nationwide (United States); **4, 5.** CBS News/MarketWatch Poll, December 17–19, 1999, 1,026 adults nationwide (United States)

UNIT 33

Exercise 6B People's Choice Awards

Read the information below. Use your own words to tell your partner how winners of the People's Choice Awards are determined. Use complete sentences and speak smoothly: Stress content words but not function words.

Nomination and Selection Process: Nominations and winners are not selected by people in the motion picture industry; a Gallup poll samples the general public; people are asked their opinions about their favorite movies and movie stars of the year; the people who are polled are free to name any star/movie that they like (for that year); since 1999, the public has been allowed to vote for a few of the awards on the Internet.

UNIT 37

Exercise 4 The Place Name Game

1. Andes Mountains (continent)
2. Mississippi River (country)
3. Nile River (continent)
4. Mount Everest (country/countries)
5. Tokyo (country)
6. Hollywood (state)
7. Beijing (country)
8. United Nations headquarters (city)
9. Golden Gate Bridge (city)
10. Taj Mahal [taʒ məhal] (country)

Answers:

1. in South America **2.** in the United States **3.** in Africa **4.** between Nepal and Tibet **5.** in Japan **6.** in California **7.** in China **8.** in New York **9.** in San Francisco **10.** in India

UNIT 40

Exercise 4 Riddles

Read the riddles to your partner, speaking smoothly and clearly. If your partner can't guess the answer, give hints.

1. What is better than the best and worse than the worst? Answer: nothing.
2. You want to share it if you have it, but if you share it, you don't have it. What is it? Answer: a secret.
3. Why are 2001 American dollar bills worth more than 1999 American dollar bills? Answer: Because $2,001 is more than $1,999.

UNIT 41

Exercise 5 Beliefs

Read these past beliefs to your partner. Introduce the sentence with "People used to believe that . . ." and change the verb in the sentence to the past tense. Reduce *that* and pronounce the sounds in *that the* carefully. Your partner will state the current belief.

1. The earth is the center of the universe.
2. The sun goes around the earth.
3. The character of a person can be seen in the shape of the head. (This was an early theory of psychology, called *phrenology.*)
4. The first two people on earth were Adam and Eve.

UNIT 46

Exercise 4 Jeopardy

When you are the contestant, choose a category and an amount. After you hear the clue, ask a question that the clue answers.

Category 1: Bodies of Water (rivers, lakes, oceans, seas)	Category 2: Countries
100	100
200	200
300	300
400	400

When you are the host, read these clues:

Category 3: States	Category 4: Continents
100 Clue: Miami, Disney World, the Everglades (Answer: What is Florida?)	100 Clue: France, Portugal, Austria (Answer: What is Europe?)
200 Clue: San Antonio, the Alamo, Houston (Answer: What is Texas?)	200 Clue: Brazil, Peru, Uruguay (Answer: What is South America?)
300 Clue: Sacramento, Silicon Valley, the Golden Gate Bridge (Answer: What is California?)	300 Clue: the Great Wall, Bangkok, Mongolia (Answer: What is Asia?)
400 Clue: Harvard, Beacon Hill, Cape Cod (Answer: What is Massachusetts?)	400 Clue: Cairo, Lagos, Nairobi (Answer: What is Africa?)

APPENDIX II: for team 2 players

UNIT 1

Exercise 5 Fill in the grid

Do not show your partner your grid. Ask your partner questions to complete your grid: for example, "What's in box *A1*?" When you have both completed your grids, compare them. They should be the same.

	1	2	3	4
A		filled	field	ten
B	waste		tan	tin
C	west			ton
D				

UNIT 2

Exercise 5 Fill in the grid

Do not show your partner your grid. Ask your partner questions to complete your grid: for example, "What's in box *A1*?" When you have both completed your grids, compare them. They should be the same.

	1	2	3	4
A		mill	meal	
B	risen	reason		greed
C				grid
D	cheek			chick

UNIT 4

Exercise 2 The [æ]-[ɛ] Game

1. What's another word for "slim"?
2. What's a word that means "not present or future"?
3. People who want to lose weight should eat foods low in ____________.
4. What word describes food that doesn't have much flavor?
5. Your head sits on this part of your body.
6. What's the past tense of "flee"?
7. What's the opposite of "cried"?
8. Add this color to red and you'll get orange.
9. What's the word for a baby cow?
10. What's the name of a yellow fruit that's long and curved, and white on the inside?

Answers:

1. slender **2.** past **3.** fat/calories **4.** bland **5.** neck **6.** fled **7.** laughed **8.** yellow **9.** calf **10.** banana

UNIT 5

Exercise 6A Can't Buy Me Love

Read these statements to your partner. Your partner will decide which intangible money is being used to buy.

1. I'm good to my employees. I've just upgraded their health insurance, and I help them out whenever I can. I stand by them, and I expect them to stand by me.
2. I take my friends out to clubs all the time. I have a good time and I know they do. I like spending my money on people; I know they like it, too. I never have any trouble finding people to do things with.
3. If I win the lottery, I'm going to quit my job. Nobody's ever going to tell me what to do again.

UNIT 6

Exercise 2 Fill in the Grid

Do not show your grid to your partner. Ask your partner questions to complete your grid; for example, "What's in box *A1*?" When you both complete your grids, compare them. They should be the same.

	1	2	3	4
A		rut	sacks	
B	sex	hem		rot
C		sucks		
D	socks			ham

UNIT 7

Exercise 6 Jeopardy: Firsts

Start as the contestant: Choose an amount: 100, 200, 300, 400, or 500. When your partner reads you the clue, say the *question* that the clue answers.

Host role: When your partner selects an amount, read the clue for that amount. Your partner must guess the *question.* Pronounce *first* correctly.

100: These people were the first inhabitants of North America.
200: The first Olympics were in this country.
300: This man was the first president of the United States.
400: This was the first woman to win a Nobel Prize.
500: This country was the first to send a person into space.

[Who are Native Americans/American Indians? What is Greece? Who was George Washington? Who was Marie Curie? What was the Soviet Union?]

UNIT 10

Exercise 4 The [ɑy]-[aw]-[oy] Game

1. What word means "a lot of people in one place"?
2. When a fruit is ready to eat, it's ________.
3. What's the opposite of "public"?
4. What do you use to cut meat?
5. This word means that you suspect something is not true.
6. What do children play with (a general name)?
7. What's the noun for "proud"?
8. What's a synonym for "bothered"?
9. What's the opposite of "then"?
10. Schoolchildren learn to add, subtract, multiply, and ________.

Answers:

1. crowd(ed) **2.** ripe **3.** private **4.** a knife **5.** doubt **6.** toys **7.** pride **8.** annoyed **9.** now **10.** divide

UNIT 11

Exercise 4 Fill in the Grid

Do not show your partner your grid. Ask your partner questions to complete your grid: for example, "What's in box *A1*?" When you both complete your grids, compare them. They should be the same.

	1	2	3	4
A			very	berry
B			rate	
C	west	vest	late	
D			breathe	breeze

UNIT 14

Exercise 4 The TH Game

1. The word "parents" refers to your ________ and ________
2. What's the opposite of "rough" or "bumpy"?
3. What should you say when someone does something nice for you?
4. What's a word that means "a way (of doing something)"?
5. What's the term for the hide (skin) of a cow that is used to make shoes?

6. Someone who writes a book is an ________.
7. What's the plural of "that"?
8. What preposition do you use with tunnels?
9. When you want to ask about the value of something, you say "How much ________?"
10. What's the name of the science of numbers?
11. What's the name of the day you were born?
12. What's an adverb that means carefully and completely?
13. What's the name of the day that follows Wednesday?
14. What's the name of the upper part of the leg, above the knee?

Answers:
1. mother and father **2.** smooth
3. thank you/thanks **4.** method **5.** leather
6. author **7.** those **8.** through **9.** is it worth
10. math(ematics) **11.** birthday **12.** thoroughly
13. Thursday **14.** thigh

UNIT 15

Exercise 5 Box Office Hits

Top-Grossing Movies Worldwide* (from release to 9/2002)			
Rank	**Title**	**Year released**	**Box office earnings**
1			
2	*Harry Potter and the Sorcerer's Stone*	2001	$966,000,000**
3			
4	*Jurassic Park*	1993	$920,000,000
5	*Lord of the Rings: The Fellowship of the Ring*	2001	$860,000,000
6	*Independence Day*	1996	$811,000,000
7			
8			
9	*The Lion King*	1994	$768,000,000
10			

*Source: www.us.imdb.com, 9/17/02
** Say "nine hundred sixty-six million dollars."

UNIT 19

Exercise 6A Arguing Styles

	You	Your partner
1. Do you apologize for things you haven't done or said to end an argument?	Usually ☐ Sometimes ☐ Rarely ☐	Usually ☐ Sometimes ☐ Rarely ☐
2. If you realize you were wrong during the course of the argument, do you admit it?	Usually ☐ Sometimes ☐ Rarely ☐	Usually ☐ Sometimes ☐ Rarely ☐
3. Do you prefer to have a friend or relative around when you argue (as a "judge")?	Usually ☐ Sometimes ☐ Rarely ☐	Usually ☐ Sometimes ☐ Rarely ☐
4. When you argue about something current, do you bring up past unresolved issues in your relationship?	Usually ☐ Sometimes ☐ Rarely ☐	Usually ☐ Sometimes ☐ Rarely ☐
5. After you argue, are you left with bitter feelings?	Usually ☐ Sometimes ☐ Rarely ☐	Usually ☐ Sometimes ☐ Rarely ☐
6. Do you tell your partner what you don't like about his/her behavior?	Usually ☐ Sometimes ☐ Rarely ☐	Usually ☐ Sometimes ☐ Rarely ☐
7. Do you ask your partner what he/she doesn't like about your behavior?	Usually ☐ Sometimes ☐ Rarely ☐	Usually ☐ Sometimes ☐ Rarely ☐
8. Do you get so furious during arguments that you can't think clearly?	Usually ☐ Sometimes ☐ Rarely ☐	Usually ☐ Sometimes ☐ Rarely ☐

UNIT 20

Exercise 6 Immigration Quiz
Your partner will read you the first two questions. Select your answers from these choices:

1. a. 22.7 percent **b.** 16 percent **c.** 8.5 percent
2. a. 38 million **b.** 28 million **c.** 55 million

Ask your partner these questions. Your partner has the choices for each question. Give your partner information about both correct and incorrect answers.

continued

3. In 2000, 26 percent of Americans born in the United States had a bachelor's degree or higher. What proportion of all foreign-born Americans had a bachelor's degree or higher?*
   a. 45 percent. Incorrect. This was the percent for Americans born in Asia.
   b. 26 percent. Correct.
   c. 22 percent. Incorrect. This is the percent of foreign-born who had less than a ninth-grade education.
4. People born in Latin America made up the largest proportion of the foreign-born population in 1999: 51 percent. What was the proportion born in Asia?*
   a. 34 percent. Incorrect. This was the proportion for people born in Central America.
   b. 26 percent. Correct.
   c. 15 percent. Incorrect. This is the proportion for people born in Europe.

*Information from the U.S. Census Bureau, 2000 http://www.census.gov

UNIT 21

Exercise 6 The Love Poll

	You	Your Partner	1999 Poll (%) Women	Men
4. Have you ever cheated on a person you were in a relationship with?				
a. Yes	___	___	17%	26%
b. No	___	___	80	72
c. Won't say	___	___	3	2
5. How do you think most men feel about Valentine's Day?				
a. They dread it.	___	___	53%	38%
b. They look forward to it.	___	___	29	42
c. Not sure	___	___	18	20
6. Which phrase describes your love life?				
a. Very happy	___	___	59%	62%
b. Could be happier	___	___	19	23
c. What love life?	___	___	17	12
d. Not sure	___	___	5	3

UNIT 22

Exercise 5 Quotations with Dark L

Quote 3

a. the past tense of "tell"
b. a future auxiliary verb
c. the present of *a.*
d. the same as *b.*
e. the opposite of "native"; a word that rhymes with "Warren"

Quote 4

a. the opposite of "young"; a word that rhymes with "cold"
b. a word that means "all the time"; a word that rhymes with "hallways"
c. a plural word that sounds similar to "comical"; a word that starts like "chronic" and ends with a dark l
d. the same as *a.*

Answers:

Quote 3: **a.** told **b.** will **c.** tell **d.** will **e.** foreign
Quote 4: **a.** old **b.** always **c.** chronicles **d.** old

UNIT 29

Exercise 5 College Courses

Aks your partner questions to complete the transcript.

Fall Semester 2004	Grade	Course description
Engl3972	B+	English 3972. Upward Mobility Stories. This seminar will deal with "rags-to-riches" or "upward mobility" stories in twentieth-century American novels. It will explore the reasons for the popularity of these stories as well as the complex cultural issues they involve.
GenS2602	A	Genetic Science 2602. Methods in Genetics and Development. This course surveys a variety of laboratory methods used in genetics research. Students will rotate through the major labs of the department.
Econ3015		
ArtH3042		

UNIT 30

Exercise 4 Trivia

Ask your partner these questions. Your partner will guess the answer. Say "higher" or "lower" until your partner guesses the correct percentage.

1. What percent of people thought Elvis Presley was the greatest rock star of all time? (about 40%)
2. What percent of people thought China would become the greatest world power in the twenty-first century? (16%)
3. What percent of people felt that gasoline-powered cars would be out-of-date by the end of the twenty-first century? (70%)
4. What percent of people said that their greatest hope for the next century was a cure for deadly diseases like cancer or AIDS? (13%)
5. Of the possible developments for the twenty-first century, what percent of people felt that human cloning would be the worst? (about 60%)

Sources: **1.** ABC News Poll, August 7–11, 2002, 1,023 adults nationwide (United States); **2.** Shell Oil Company Shell Poll, November 5–8, 1998, 1,264 adults nationwide (United States); **3.** CBS News/MarketWatch Poll, December 17–19, 1999, 1,026 adults nationwide (United States); **4.** ABC News Poll, August 16–22, 1999, 506 adults nationwide (United States); **5.** Shell Oil Company Shell Poll, November 5–8, 1998, 1,264 adults nationwide (United States)

UNIT 33

Exercise 6B Academy Awards

Read the information below. Use your own words to tell your partner how winners of the Academy Awards are determined. Use complete sentences and speak smoothly: Stress content words but not function words.

Membership: 5,816 voting members (as of 2004); membership limited to distinguished individuals in motion pictures; members belong to one of 14 branches: actors, art directors, cinematographers, directors, documentaries, executives, editors, music, producers, public relations, short films and animation, sound, visual effects, and writers.

Nomination Process: Members within a branch nominate films or individuals for awards related to their branch; in some categories, such as best foreign film, nominations are made by large committees made up of members from all branches; Best Picture nominees come from the entire voting membership; the top five nominees are presented for voting.

Voting Process: Most final winners are determined by a vote of the entire membership.

UNIT 37

Exercise 4 The Place Name Game

1. Alps (continent)
2. Eiffel Tower (city)
3. Great Wall of China (continent)
4. Miami (country)
5. Kremlin (city)
6. Sears Tower (city)
7. Hawaiian Islands (ocean)
8. Sahara Desert (continent)
9. Empire State Building (city)
10. Amazon River (continent)

Answers:

1. in Europe **2.** in Paris **3.** in Asia **4.** in the United States **5.** in Moscow **6.** in Chicago **7.** in the Pacific Ocean **8.** in Africa **9.** in New York **10.** in South America

UNIT 40

Exercise 4 Riddles

Read the riddles to your partner, speaking smoothly and clearly. If your partner can't guess the answer, give hints.

1. The poor have it; the rich need it, and if you eat it, you'll die. What is it? Answer: nothing.
2. You destroy me if you name me. What am I? Answer: silence.
3. Even if it's starving, an Arctic polar bear will never eat a penguin egg. Why? Answer: Penguins live in Antarctica.

UNIT 41

Exercise 5 Beliefs

Your partner will read some past beliefs to you. Tell your partner the current belief.

Then, read these past beliefs to your partner. Introduce the sentence with "People used to believe that . . ." and change the verb in the sentence to the past tense. Reduce *that* and pronounce the sounds in *that the* carefully. Your partner will state the current belief.

1. The four basic substances of the universe are earth, air, fire, and water.
2. The spirits of the dead continue to live in animals.
3. The world is flat.
4. The world is held up by Atlas, a very strong man.

UNIT 46

Exercise 4 Jeopardy

When you are the host, read these clues:

Category 1: Bodies of Water	Category 2: Countries
100 Clue: the Pacific, the Atlantic, the Arctic (Answer: What are oceans?)	100 Clue: Toronto, Vancouver, Quebec (Answer: What is Canada?)
200 Clue: the Mediter-ranean, the Baltic, the Caribbean (Answer: What are seas?)	200 Clue: Kyoto, Tokyo, Hiroshima (Answer: What is Japan?)
300 Clue: the Nile, the Hudson, the Yangtze (Answer: What are rivers?)	300 Clue: Berlin, Frankfurt, Munich (Answer: What is Germany?)
400 Clue: Michigan, Tahoe, Victoria (Answer: What are lakes?)	400 Clue: Sydney, Adelaide, Melbourne (Answer: What is Australia?)

When you are the contestant, choose a category and an amount. After you hear the clue, ask a question that the clue answers.

Category 3: States	Category 4: Continents
100	100
200	200
300	300
400	400

APPENDIX III: spelling patterns and silent letters

SPELLING PATTERNS

The chart below presents common and uncommon spellings of vowels and selected consonants. Though consonant sounds can usually be predicted from the spelling, most vowel sounds can be spelled in several different ways. It is important to be aware of both the common and uncommon spellings for vowel sounds.

VOWELS

Sound	Common spellings		Less common spellings	
[iy]	*ee*	three, freeze	*ey*	key, donkey
	e . . e (silent *e*)	these, complete	*ei*	receive, ceiling
	e	me, even, recent	*i*	ski, machine
	ea	tea, leaf	*eo*	people
	ie	piece, believe		
[ɪ]	*i*	six, picture	*e*	English, pretty
	y	gym, system	*ui*	build, guilty
			u	busy, business
			o	women
[ey]	*a . . e* (silent *e*)	taste, plate	*eigh*	eight, weight
	a	paper, baby	*ea*	break, great
	ai	wait, praise	*ey*	they, obey
	ay	pay, stay	*ei*	veil, vein
[ɛ]	*e*	tennis, seven, left	*ea*	dead, breakfast
			a	many, any
			ai	said, again
			ay	says
			ie	friend
[æ]	*a*	that, glasses	*au*	laugh, aunt
			ai	plaid

Sound	Common spellings		Less common spellings	
[ə] (stressed) (As an unstressed vowel sound, [ə] can be spelled with any vowel.)	*u*	bus, husband	*ou*	country, young
	o	money, come	*oo*	blood, flood
			oe	does, doesn't
			a	what, was
[ɑ]	*o*	block, probably	*ow*	knowledge
	a	father, start	*ear*	heart
			er	sergeant
[uw]	*oo*	balloon, boot	*o*	do, move
	oo . . e (silent *e*)	choose, loose	*ou*	group, soup
	u	student, truth, rule	*ough*	through
			ew	flew, new
			ui	suit, juice
[ʊ]	*oo*	good, book	*ou*	could, should
	u	pull, push	*o*	woman, wolf
[ow]	*o . . . e* (silent *e*)	joke, explode	*oe*	toe, Joe
	o	go, open	*ough*	dough, although
	oa	road, boat	*ew*	sew
	ow	grow, know		
[ɔ]	*au*	pause, fault	*ough*	bought, thought
	aw	law, dawn	*oa*	broad
	a (before *l*)	fall, call		
	o	loss, strong		
[ɑy]	*i . . e* (silent *e*)	time, invite	*uy*	buy, guy
	i	Friday, mind	*eigh*	height
	igh	high, light	*ai*	aisle
	y	cry, apply	*ey*	eye
	ie	die, lie		
[aw]	*ou*	surround, house	*ough*	bough, drought
	ow	crowd, allow		
[oy]	*oi*	voice, noise		
	oy	toy, employ		

SELECTED CONSONANTS

Sound	Common spellings		Less common spellings	
[s]	*s*	sister, last	*sc*	muscle, scene
	ss	boss, address	*ce*	receive, cent
	se	house, purpose	*ci*	city, acid
			sw (silent *w*)	answer, sword
[z]	*z*	zoo, zipper	*ss*	dessert, possess
	s (between vowels)	reason, present		
	se	please, rise		
[ʃ]	*sh*	shower, cash	*ss*	pressure, issue
	ti	patient, nation	*su*	sugar, insure
	ci	special, physician	*si*	dimension
	ssi	profession, permission		
[ʒ]	*si*	decision, occasion	*ti*	equation
	ge	beige, massage	*zu*	seizure, azure
	su	leisure, treasure		

SILENT LETTERS

Silent *p* ~~p~~sychology, ~~p~~sychiatrist, ~~p~~sychic, ~~p~~neumonia, recei~~p~~t, cor~~p~~s, cu~~p~~board
Silent *b* clim~~b~~, thum~~b~~, lam~~b~~, com~~b~~, dou~~b~~t, de~~b~~t, su~~b~~tle
Silent *t* lis~~t~~en, whis~~t~~le, cas~~t~~le, of~~t~~en, mus~~t~~n't, balle~~t~~, vale~~t~~, mor~~t~~gage
Silent *d* We~~d~~nesday, han~~d~~some, han~~d~~kerchief
Silent *k* ~~k~~now, ~~k~~nowledge, ~~k~~not, ~~k~~nee, ~~k~~nife
Silent *g* ~~g~~nat, ~~g~~naw, ~~g~~narl, ~~g~~nash, ~~g~~nocchi
Silent *s* ai~~s~~le, i~~s~~land, corp~~s~~
Silent *h* ~~h~~onor, ~~h~~onest, ~~h~~eir, ex~~h~~ibit, ex~~h~~aust, ve~~h~~icle (see also Unit 24)
Silent *l* cou~~l~~d, wou~~l~~d, shou~~l~~d, wa~~l~~k, ta~~l~~k, cha~~l~~k, ca~~l~~m, pa~~l~~m, sa~~l~~mon, yo~~l~~k, ha~~l~~f, ca~~l~~f
Silent *w* ~~w~~rite, ~~w~~rong, ans~~w~~er, s~~w~~ord